WITHHOLD NOT
CORRECTION

WITHHOLD NOT CORRECTION

Bruce A. Ray

Presbyterian & Reformed Publishing Company
Phillipsburg, New Jersey 08865

To
My Dear Wife
and Children
Who
Have Turned Theory
Into Practice
and
Who Make Home
a
Nice Place
To Be

Contents

Foreword

This book offers a salutary correction to the many errone-
ous views of child training on the market today. Parents and
Christian educators should welcome its publication. In
Ephesians 6, Paul quotes the children's commandment and
notes that it is the first commandment with a promise ("that
your days may be long in the land"). The importance of holding before children proper incentives for genuine achievement
must not be underestimated. Yet the promise also implies a
threat (If you dishonor and disobey your father and mother,
your days will be shortened). A rebellious child was put to
death in Israel; there was no juvenile delinquency problem.

Moreover, in this passage Paul, with characteristic balance,
stresses disciplining children both in the "nurture and admonition [discipline with teeth and personal confrontation]
of the Lord" (v.4). That means that they must be brought to
the point of obedience by the rod if necessary, but that they
must also always be confronted about their obligation to
obey because of the Lord and because of the death of Christ
for His people. More and more, after conversion, their desire
should shift from threat of punishment to a desire to please
the Lord Who loved them enough to give His life for them.

Because this book exalts Christ and His Word, I commend
it to you and hope that it will be the source of much blessing.

Jay Adams

Introduction

Books on baby and child care are readily available in most supermarkets and drugstores. There are many medically-oriented paperbacks that will tell you how to treat common illnesses or emergencies and how to train your children to be physically strong and mentally awake. Psychology has become a very fertile field for publishing, and these specialists are rapidly adding their observations and insights to the shelves of bookstores. Why another book on training children? Because the Christian parent needs more. He needs to know how to raise his children to be morally straight and spiritually alive. He needs to know how to bring them up in a manner that will be pleasing to God.

I am not a medical doctor; nor am I a psychologist. I *am* a father and a pastor, and I bring that perspective to the question of training children. For me the Scripture is the standard of truth in this and in every other area of life. This is not to deny the contributions of physicians and psychologists. I buy their paperbacks so that I can know what to expect from my three-year-old, or what to do when one of our children develops a rash. But it *is* to say that in order to be useful their works must be made subject to the Word of God. The doctor sees the birth experience in terms of biological processes, safe procedures, and possible complications. The psychologist sees it as a traumatic experience for the woman who has gone through the ordeal of labor, for the infant who has changed environments, and for the husband who got the bill! But for us who know the Lord, the birth of a child is an experience that is a spiritual as well as a biological and psychological event! We know that children are a gift from the Lord.

Becoming a parent is a very exciting and rewarding experience, but *being* a parent is much more enduring. The gift of a child to a man and a woman forever changes their status: they are no longer just husband and wife, but they are now entitled to that wonderful word, *parents.* The glory and the glamor of having a new baby around the house will begin to diminish within just a few months, but the *responsibilities* attached to that word *parent* will remain as long as we are alive. Old Eli was responsible for the conduct of his sons even though he was very old and they were full-grown men. The Bible says that judgment was brought upon his house by God "because his sons made themselves vile, and he restrained them not."

Parents, then, have not only a full-time job, but a lifetime job! And yet, although it will occupy all our days, this is a job for which we generally receive little if any practical preparation. We either resolve to bring up our children in the same way in which we were raised, or else (reacting against the methods of our parents) we determine to bring them up according to the most up-to-date popular paperback we can find.

But is either approach *really* satisfactory? Were our parents always right (or always wrong) in their approach to training children? And should the methods of our mothers and fathers serve as absolute standards of right and wrong for what *we* do in trying to fulfill our calling as Christian parents before the Lord?

The Christian is called to live out every aspect of his life in obedience to the revealed will of God. This means that God, who gives us children, has in His Word also told us how we should regard the children He has given us and how we should bring them up in a way that will please Him.

What *is* a child, anyway? Who is this squirmy little creature who captures our hearts and who so drastically changes our lives? Our answer to this question must necessarily have a decisive effect upon the methods we use in raising our children. If, for example, we believe with one popular psychologist that our children are simply a higher form of animal, the product of evolutionary *chance,* then we may justly employ the same methods used successfully by the *Ace Obedience School* to train German shepherds. Behavioral manipulation may then be acceptable, if this is true. But if the psychologist we have chosen to follow is *wrong* in his understanding of the nature of children, if our children are something *more* than intelligent animals, then the price we'll pay will be enormous in terms of the spiritual-emotional violence that we will perpetrate against our own offspring as they grow into adulthood.

If, again, we presuppose that children are by nature *innocent* (without guilt or personal sin) until they reach some rather vague *age of accountability,* then how can we account for the anger, frustration, and selfishness that are apparent even from the earliest days? More importantly, what instruction can we give to our children to help them to rightly handle the anger and frustration that they experience daily if we assume that they are not sinners? Must we stand by and helplessly watch while our children do themselves spiritual and even bodily harm trying to cope with the hard realities of life? No, say some of the family-experts, we can leave the room until the tantrum is over and then try to divert his attention to some other activity. Is this our calling as parents?

To just stand around with our hands in our pockets and wait to pick up the pieces? Or are we called to have a more formative influence upon our children, to guide them and direct them into the proper path? How can we know?

God has told us in his Word that He made us (male and female) in His image. This means that our children, too, are bearers of the image of God. Consequently, we must reject every methodology that would urge us to treat our children as if they were only intelligent animals. But this approach to discipline is quite common today, and has even been "baptized" into the faith by certain Christian psychologists. If we are to fulfill our calling as Christian parents, we must interpret our children in the full light of what God has said about them and not in the vague shadows of what modern men think.

We and our children are bearers of the image of God. But the image that we now bear is not a true image: it is distorted. Adam, acting as the natural and federal head of the race of men, by one act of rebellion plunged all mankind into a state of sin and misery (Gen. 3). Now the image that we bear as Adam's descendants is like his after the fall, fractured and distorted (Gen. 5:1-3). Instead of being a true reflection, it is like the grotesque images seen in the curved mirrors of a carnival side show. This, too, must affect the way in which we regard our children and the methods that we use to discipline them. We must *correct* them; we must strive to *bring them back* to their proper path as image-bearers of God. If we regard them as *innocent,* and not as distorted, we will not correct them and we will fail in our calling as Christian parents.

Biblical correction holds out tremendous hope to us as mothers and fathers. The parents of an adopted four-year-old rebel who also had physical disabilities wrote to say that as they began to apply biblical principles of correction consistently, their daughter's personality changed 99%. She began to obey them, peace entered into their home, and love was at last able to flow freely in both directions.

Prospective parents, young parents, parents with older children, and even grandparents need to know what God says in His Word about the correction of children. Indeed, everyone who is in any way related to children must learn to discipline them according to the will of God. Aunts, uncles, teachers, and even babysitters will find a survey of the biblical data to be of great value.

But where can detailed instruction of this nature be found? Sometimes there is a chapter on discipline tucked away deep in the recesses of some monumental work on the Christian home or family, but at most there are only a few pages devoted to the actual application of correction and at best only a few obvious principles are considered.

As Christian parents we need to ask ourselves a number of questions that other parents don't ask. Why do my children need to be corrected? What is my objective or goal in disciplining them, what am I trying to achieve? How does God say I should correct my children? How can I fulfill my responsibility as a parent before the Lord in a way that will see my children brought to the feet of Jesus Christ?

Some time ago in our church we spent a summer trying to answer these questions. We looked to the Scriptures, the authoritative revelation of the will of God, to tell us how to order our lives and our homes. The pages that follow reflect the answers that we found and have begun to apply.

As a young pastor and father I send this book forth as an attempt to deal in a biblical and practical way with only a small part of the enormous task of raising our children in a way that will bring honor and glory to the Name of our God. I am very thankful for the encouragement I have received from pastors and parents in other churches and conferences where I have spoken. Several pastors have even made the reading of this book in its previous form a regular part of their pre-marital counseling strategy.

So many have entered into my labors that it would be impossible to acknowledge everyone who has assisted in the production of this book. My co-laborers include the men, women, and children of the Reformed Baptist Church in Wilmington, Delaware, and of the Juanita Community Church in Kirkland, Washington. I am especially indebted to Dr. Jay Adams, whose writings and example have challenged me to attempt to think through this issue biblically. *To God be the glory, Amen.*

Bruce A. Ray
Kirkland, Washington
January, 1978

PROVERBS 23:13-14 (AV)*

Withhold not correction from the child: for if thou beatest him with the rod, he shall not die.

Thou shalt beat him with the rod, and shalt deliver his soul from hell.

*All biblical quotations are from the New American Standard Bible (©The Lockman Foundation) unless otherwise noted.

1

Knowing Our Children

The sun was hot against my shoulder as we drove north on California's Golden State Freeway (I-5). I was glad for the air-conditioning in our '66 Impala. We left the freeway at Castaic, and soon eased into a parking space in front of a row of neat little yellow stucco houses. As I opened her door my wife got out, holding in her arms our most precious possession. "Welcome home, son, on your very first day out of the hospital."

His name is Nathaniel—that's the name we gave to him, and it means *gift of God.* But as I carried in the little blue suitcase, I couldn't help wondering, "Who are you?"

He seems as fragile as a new flower, but he's really as strong as steel. He's flesh of my flesh, and yet he's his own flesh. He's the product of our loving union, and yet he is distinct from both of us. What actually *is* a child, anyway? Do you know?

That may sound a little foolish. After all, you've known your child since before he was born. You mothers carried him for nine months, and felt his first feeble movements within. You've fed, burped, changed, and bathed him for years. You know his likes and his dislikes, his allergies, his habits. You know him better than anyone else *could*. But do you know him as God does?

Your child is made in the image of God.

The *image of God* is that which makes man different from the animals and uniquely man. Scientists have sometimes lumped man and the animals into the same category because there are certain biological and chemical similarities, but this is biblically wrong. Man is made in the image of God; the animals are not. The origin and the essence of man are quite different, and man is not simply a *higher form* of animal. It was *after* the creation of plant and animal life that God said, "Let Us make man in Our image, according to Our likeness; and let them rule over the fish of the sea and over the birds of the sky and over the cattle and over all the earth, and over every creeping thing that creeps on the earth" (Gen. 1:26). As man came from the hand of God he was specially created (Gen. 2:7), and enjoyed a unique relationship as God's vice-regent upon the earth. This cannot be said of the animals. "And God created man in His own image, in the image of God He created him; male and female He created them" (Gen. 1:27).

But what does it mean, to bear the image of God? This term is theologically so heavy-laden that we are tempted to miss the simplicity of it. We all know what images are: we look at one every morning in the bathroom mirror. What I see there is not *me;* it is an *image,* a *reflection,* of what I look like. There are some very obvious similarities, and there are some very important differences. The *image of me* and I look alike—we have the same hair, the same eyes, and the same nose holding up our glasses. But when I raise my right hand, the *image of me* raises its *left* hand! I have flesh and blood and weight; the *image of me* is as thin as a sheet of glass, and doesn't even register on the scale! And when I walk away into another room, the *image of me* cannot come along. We are in some respects similar; but we are at the same time very different.

Now let me sketch in some ideas that will suggest what it means for us to be made in the image of God. The following list is not exhaustive: it is meant only to be suggestive.

1. God is the eternal I AM; man is a self-conscious being. Philosophers may struggle with questions about existence, but God does not. And, except in the classroom, neither do we. We all know that we are, that we do exist, and we all have consciousness of *self.* In this we are a reflection of God, the eternal I AM. Our children give early expression to their self-consciousness when they begin to talk. Words such as *me, mine,* or *my* are favorites in a toddler's vocabulary.

2. God is the eternal *logos,* the Word; man is a rational being. *Word* speaks of the structure of thought. Man has a mind, and can think with it.

3. God can communicate His thoughts to men, another side of *Word;* men can also communicate, both with God and with other men. Children soon learn to communicate their thoughts and desires by making sounds. You know when your baby isn't very happy. Soon gestures are added to sounds, to add emphasis and to be more specific. A grunt or two with the index finger pointing to the cookie jar leaves no doubt about what Johnny wants. Add a few skills, such as writing, and we can see how man reflects God the Word.

4. God is the Creator; man has creative ability. Technically, the term *create* ought to be reserved for God, who brought into existence all things from nothing. Man cannot do that. Man can take existing materials and place them into new relationships. This is not really creating; it is manufacturing. Nevertheless, in common language we talk about someone's *creativity.* Children place blocks together in new relationships, building walls, towers, and whole cities. Scribbling progresses to recognizable and intentional geometric

forms, and with a little bit of color *everyone* is pleased with Susie's *creation*. In her art work, Susie is reflecting the activity of God in creating the world with all its shapes and colors.

5. God is sovereign and possesses *all authority;* man exercises dominion over the earth. Why do you suppose that children like having pets—all kinds of pets? It's not only because they're warm and cuddly (not all are), but also because, as image-bearers of God, they are intended to reflect His sovereignty over the Animal Kingdom (Gen. 1:26).

6. God is altogether righteous; man is a moral being responsible for his actions. Man cannot escape the force of conscience alternately accusing or else defending him. Children are moral beings who can and must learn right from wrong.

7. God is eternal and omnipresent; man is bound to time and space. Or is he? What about the gift of imagination? Children playing are not wasting time—they are experiencing a touch of eternity. When they're playing, children can be *whatever they want to be* (fireman, cowboy, doctor or nurse) *whenever they want to be* (old west or future city) *wherever they want to be* (Texas or Mars). They escape the boundaries of time and space in their imaginations, and thus reflect the eternality and omnipresence of God.

Children are indeed wonderful gifts from the Lord. They are little image-bearers created by Him for His own glory. We receive them from His hand as His reward. How well do we really *know* them?

REVIEW

1. How can we know what children are in God's sight?
2. What does the phrase *image of God* mean?
3. In what ways do children reflect the glory of God?

RESPONSE

1. How do I look upon my little   (your child's name) ?
2. Do I show respect toward my children as unique persons?
3. Do I see them as bearing the image of God in the same way that I do?
4. In what ways can I change my attitude toward my children to be obedient to the Scriptures?

2

The Biblical Necessity
for Correction

If children are made in the image of God, then why is it necessary for us to correct them? Why don't they just naturally do what's right as image-bearers? Why does God in the Scriptures command all parents to discipline their children, saying, "Withhold not correction from the child. . ." (Prov. 23:13 AV)? If we can discover in the Scriptures *why* discipline is *necessary*, that ought to be sufficient reason to compel us to search out a manner of correction that will be pleasing to God and beneficial to our children according to His Word. Biblically there are at least four factors which make the exercise of correction an absolute necessity in the home that would be Christian. In this chapter we want to examine those factors.

First, the nature of the child demands correction. Philosophers of this world have been telling us for centuries that children are born innocent; that is, without sin and without guilt. Perhaps it was the philosopher *John Locke* who gave us the clearest expression of this idea in his *Essay Concerning Human Understanding,* first published in 1690. Locke said that at birth the mind of every individual is a *tabula rasa,* or a blank tablet, to be written upon by environment and experience. The child is born neutral: without experience, without morality, without ideas, without concepts. It remains for society to place its imprint upon that blank tablet and thereby create the kind of character that society wants to see in that innocent child. Thus when the President of the United States, John F. Kennedy, was gunned down in the streets of Dallas, it was not the man who fired from a nearby building who was to blame. It was society. When Martin Luther King was shot while standing on a balcony in Memphis, it was not the sniper who was at fault. Radio, television, and the press all led us into a period of national agony. What kind of society, they wailed, could create an environment where such things can happen? Again, when Robert Kennedy was murdered before live television cameras in Los Angeles and when George Wallace was wounded in Maryland, society was accused, tried, and found guilty of these bloody crimes. After all, the gunmen in all of these instances were once little babies bouncing on somebody's knee. They were innocent children born with blank tablets. It was society that shaped them, and it must be society that will hang. The individual cannot be held responsible.

We in our day think that if we can only educate our children properly, inscribing the right facts or the right data upon those blank tablets, there will necessarily be an end to all crime, violence, and bloodshed. And so, consistently with this idea, we in the United States have developed the most extensive system of free public education that is to be found anywhere in the world. What has been the result? The result has been that we in America have the most educated criminals of any country in the world! So much for man's wisdom. So much for the philosophies of men without a Word from God. How very foolish they are, and blind to plain reality. But how different, how very different, is the description of our natures that the God who made us gives to us in the Scriptures.

When we turn to the Bible we discover that something very terrible happened to man made in the image of God. Man did not remain in the original righteousness in which he was created. Turning from the creation accounts to Genesis 3, we find that Adam, the first man and the representative of *all* men, rebelled against the Lord. When he sinned as our representative, he plunged the whole race of men into a state of sin and misery. Theologians call this the Fall. And that's exactly what it was. Adam fell from everything that he had before. He fell as image-bearer, as vice-regent, and as righteous man.

The effect of that fall upon man as image-bearer can be seen in Genesis 5:1-3. In the day when God created man, He made him in the likeness of God. But when fallen Adam became the father of a son, his son was made in *his* likeness (fallen), according to *his* image (fallen). Seth, the fallen son of the fallen man, bore an image that was fractured and distorted. Like the image that you see when you look into the concave and convex mirrors of a carnival fun-house, the image is identifiable, but not at all accurate. There is still some resemblance—enough to pick out the parts—but the image is a grotesque caricature of the truth. Taking some of the same categories that we looked at before, let's see how the Fall has affected the image of God in man.

1. Man's *self-consciousness* is twisted into pride, selfishness and prejudice.

2. *Reason,* instead of being used to receive God's revelation, is used to plot mischief against others and to get them into trouble.

3. *Communication* or speech is corrupted: to curse, to lie, and to abuse others with our tongues. Children are noted for their cruelty toward other children.

4. *Creativity* is turned upside down to become destructiveness. What delight some children take in tearing down, breaking, and destroying! It doesn't really matter if a toy is old or new, theirs or somebody else's. A castle is built to be knocked down.

5. *Rule* is turned into tyranny. We all know the neighborhood bully. Children soon learn to use their size and weight to promote their own advantage.

6. *Morality* is become immorality. We don't need to teach our children how to lie or to take things that don't belong to them. They are inclined toward evil and do it naturally. Our time and energy is spent trying to teach them the *right* things to do.

7. Even such a beautiful thing as *imagination* is spoiled by the Fall. Johnny uses imagination to escape responsibility for his actions: he's late for dinner because "seven bears chased me down the street and I had to wait 'til the coast was clear!"

Who are the children? They're made in the image of God. But they're not innocent. They're fallen sinners. John Locke was as wrong as wrong can be. The God who made us declares that "the intent of man's heart is evil from his youth" (Gen. 8:21). The root of evil is within. It is not in the environment. It is within the heart of man. *That tablet is not blank:* it's filled with sin, with malice, with wickedness unspeakable.

Someone may object that the word translated "youth" in Genesis 8 is a term that refers to late childhood or early manhood. It may include teenagers, but surely not little children! The Word of God does not allow us to make that escape. In Psalm 58:3 (AV) David leaves no doubt as to who is involved and where this wickedness begins. He says, "The wicked are estranged from the womb: they go astray as soon as they be born, speaking lies." "The wicked are estranged . . ."—what does that mean? It means that there is a gulf fixed between

God and man. At what point? In the womb! Not at the age
of accountability, not at 21 or 18, not at 6 or 7, not even at
birth, but in the *womb* there is an estrangement between God
and man, between God and that little babe. What is the cause
of that estrangement? What is the cause of that separation?
What is the cause of that tension? It is to be attributed to the
fact that the imagination of man's heart is evil from his
youth. It is a biblical fact that the babe even in the womb is a
sinner rebelling against God. As soon as that babe comes out
of the womb he will go astray, speaking lies. Another trans-
lation expresses it, "they do err as soon as they be born,
speaking lies." As soon as a child is capable of any physical
expression, any observable expression, it sins. When it is in
the womb you cannot see that rebellion. You can hear its
heart beat, you can feel it kicking every once in a while, but
you do not see any outward manifestations of rebellion
against God. However, as soon as it is born, the Bible says
that the infant speaks lies. Have you ever seen an infant
speak lies? I have never known an infant that could talk, but
I have known infants that can cry. Mothers have told me that
the cries of an infant are distinguishable and I think that
even we fathers can tell the difference from time to time.
We can recognize when a child is crying out of hurt and
when he is crying out of anger. Many times the new-born
infant puts forth a false cry. He cries as though he is hurt.
When mother inspects, there is nothing binding him, nothing
pricking him, his diapers are clean, there is nothing to irritate
him, and that cry which sounded like a cry of hurt was actually nothing more than a cry of anger. So the babe from its
very birth, as soon as it is capable of any sort of expression,
speaks lies. Then, too, when he begins to speak words, he
begins to speak lies. We do not have to teach our children to
lie; they do it naturally. Children who are born and brought
up in the context of the church, children whose parents

watch over them very carefully and seek to preserve them from any environment which would teach them to lie, still lie. Why? Because their natures are corrupt, and they do these things naturally.

David was a man after God's own heart, according to the Scriptures. But David was not a man after God's own heart *naturally*. He tells us in Psalm 51:5 (AV), speaking of his own experience, "Behold, I was shapen in iniquity; and in sin did my mother conceive me." What does he mean by that? Does he mean that the act of intercourse on the part of his mother was sin? No, for no place in the Bible do you find intercourse condemned as sin in the context of marriage. The sin of Genesis chapter 3 was not sex. It was a failure on the part of Adam and Eve to obey the command of God with respect to the eating of the fruit of the tree of the knowledge of good and evil. Even *before* the Fall God told them to be fruitful and to multiply, and that would necessarily involve intercourse. What David *is* saying here is that in sin he was conceived by his mother. The very moment that the sperm from the male united with the egg from the female, the very moment that the egg was fertilized, a sinner was conceived. The very moment that there was life, human life, that human being was a sinner by nature.

Then David tells us about his early experiences when he was being formed, "Behold, I was shapen in iniquity." Where was it that David was shaped? What is he talking about? It is again in the context of conception. David was shaped just as you and I were: in the womb or in the uterus of our mothers. The point that he is making is that that environment did not affect him, but as he developed within the context of that womb environment, he gained organs capable of fulfilling the sinful intentions of his heart. As his arms and his legs were formed, and as his fingers were formed on the ends of his hands, he was shaped in iniquity: fully prepared to come forth from the womb to obey the lusts of the flesh and to express his sinful nature. This is an astounding statement. It means that we are sinners not because we sin but we sin because we are by nature sinners. The Apostle Paul says that we are *by nature* children characterized by disobedience. He says that we are *by nature* dead, spiritually dead, on account of trespasses and sin. Our Lord Jesus Christ told the Pharisees and through them he told all unsaved men that however righteous they may think they are, however they may appear in the eyes of men to be, they are in fact children of the devil, sons of Satan.

Thus the very nature of the child demands correction because it is wicked and perverse, contrary both to God and to man, and full of sin. The Lord declares (Prov. 22:15) that "foolishness is bound up in the heart of a child; the rod of discipline will remove it far from him." So the nature of the child requires correction.

Secondly, the direction of the child demands correction. Children, like adults, are full of sin and the penalty for that sin is the same, spiritual death. The courts of our land may differentiate between a ten year old who stabs his father to death and a thirty year old who does the same thing, but in the eyes of God they are both murderers and they are both equally deserving of the sentence of second death, of spiritual death, of everlasting hell. That is why God tells us that we are to beat our child with a rod in order to deliver his soul from Sheol (Prov. 23:14). The direction of the child by nature is toward hell. We must understand that. We must realize that. It must influence the fervency with which we pray for our children. It must influence the diligence with which we seek to instruct them. To realize that by nature they are destined toward hell must influence the example we seek to portray before them.

Self-expression is the cry of the modern educator. We are told that we must not restrain our children, but rather we must encourage them to express themselves. But the Bible says that the *selves* that we urge them to express are sinful! Expression of the sinful *self* can only create damage and harm. Is it any wonder, then, that the same educators have found it necessary in many of our great cities to man the halls of the schools with police armed with pistols, night sticks, mace, and tear gas? Is it any wonder that in the suburbs of our land mothers are afraid to send their children to school, lest they be assaulted between classes or even in the midst of a class? Is it any wonder that in the schools of our land teachers fear for their very lives, lest they be beaten or even *killed* by their students? Is it any wonder that the school districts complain year after year and spend increasingly more of our money to replace chemistry labs that have been purposely destroyed, to replace broken windows and repair other acts of vandalism, when we encourage children to express their sinful selves? Permissiveness is not the strategy of the Scriptures: it is the strategy of the devil. J. C. Ryle, writing almost a hundred years ago, spoke to the issue of permissiveness. Ryle warned parents, saying,

> Remember children are born with a decided bias toward evil, and therefore if you let them choose for themselves, they are certain to choose wrong. The mother cannot tell what her tender infant may grow up to be—tall or short, weak or strong, wise or foolish; he may or may not be any of these—it is all uncertain. But one thing the mother can say with certainty: he will have a corrupt and sinful heart. It is natural for us to do wrong. "Foolishness," says Solomon, "is bound in the heart of a child." "A child left to himself bringeth his mother to shame." Our hearts are like the earth on which we tread; let it alone, and it is sure to bear weeds.

In Proverbs 22:6 we read, "Train up a child in the way he should go, even when he is old he will not depart from it." This verse is usually taken as a promise, and it is almost always abused by persons seeking a false comfort. Some understand it to mean this: If the child is trained properly (that is, biblically) in his youth, *he will not depart* from that training when he grows older. Now generally speaking, this statement is true. Whether the Lord regenerates him or not, the morality which has been instilled in him as a child will carry him through his adult years. But it is not the teaching of Proverbs 22:6.

Others understand the verse to mean: If a child is trained properly in his youth, but then goes astray, *he will return* to that earlier training when he is older. This is frequently the understanding of those who desire to have a false sense of comfort. We have some friends in another city who have several children. Their oldest daughter made a profession of faith when she was very young. Our friends sent her to a Christian school in another state. After she graduated from college, she turned to her parents and said, "Thanks a lot for nothing. Now that I am free, now that I am through with my education, I am going to do what *I* want to do." She has become a member of the communist party in the United States; she is living promiscuously in a commune, and she is a source of great disappointment to her parents. But her parents are not concerned or burdened about her *spiritual* condition at all. When I spoke to them about the situation and sought to give them biblical counsel, they told me that she had made a profession of faith, they had brought her up in a Christian home, and when she is older she will return. They are not afraid for her conversion. They are not praying that the Lord will do a mighty work of grace in her heart. The next in line is a boy. As he grew up, also in the context of the church, he made a profession of faith and so forth. He married a young girl because he had made her pregnant. After he married her, he left her. He returned to her for a brief period and then left her again. Their attitude is the same in this situation: no concern. He will return when he gets older. On the basis of Proverbs 22:6 they say that God is obligated to bring him back.

These parents are just one example, but it is being multiplied by countless hundreds throughout this country because of the misunderstanding of this text. In its proper context *Proverbs 22:6 is not a promise so much as it is a warning* to Christian parents. In the *Hebrew* text of Proverbs 22:6, the phrase "in the way he should go" is entirely lacking. Rather the Hebrew says, "Train up a child *in his way* and when he is old he will not depart from it." Train up a child in *his* way or after *his* manner according to his ways. Allow a child to have self-expression, allow him to pick and to choose what he will and will not do, and as that habit is formed in his youth he will not change when he is older. If he does not learn discipline from you as a child he will never learn it as an adult. That is a warning. Or it is a promise, if you like, but it is a promise in the negative sense. If you let your children run over you, if you withhold the rod, if you fail to discipline them, if you fail to diligently and meticulously instruct them in the little things as well as the big, if you let your children decide what they will and what they will not eat, what they will and what they will not wear, what they will and what they will not do and when they will and will not do it, look into the future and you will see those same children unbridled, undisciplined, and unable to bring their bodies into submission to the commands of God. That is a stern warning. Jay Adams comments on this verse in his book *Competent to Counsel* and says, "The verse stands not as a promise but as a warning to parents that if they allow a child to train himself after his own wishes (permissively) they should not expect him to want to change these patterns when he matures. Children are born sinners and when allowed to follow their own wishes they will naturally develop sinful habit responses. The basic thought is that such habit patterns become deep-seated when they have been ingrained in the child from the earliest days." The point is that he cannot get out of the rut which you have established for him. "Train up a child in his way and when he is old he will not depart from it." To allow the child to go his own way, to allow him to take things naturally as they come, is to assure the destruction of his soul. The direction of a child, whose natural way leads to hell, demands correction.

Thirdly, the responsibility that God has placed upon us as parents demands that we correct our children. Every privilege has its corresponding responsibility. I have in my wallet a driver's license from the state of Washington. The privilege of having a driver's license requires me to maintain my vehicle in a safe condition and to have that vehicle under control whenever it is in motion. Those of you who have dogs as pets know that the privilege of possessing a pet carries with it the responsibility of restraining your animal lest a neighbor or the mailman receive bodily injury from that animal; he is your responsibility.

Children do not automatically follow a marriage license. The Bible tells us that children are a gift of God and "the fruit of the womb is a reward" (Ps. 127:3). While God may, and He does, employ *natural* processes in the begetting of children, yet in the end it is *God alone* who makes the womb barren, or who makes it fruitful. Those of you who have either tried to have children or to not have children are both, I think, aware of the fact that it is God who orders what will and what will not take place. Even the most successful of birth control methods have been known to fail. Even those parents who have most desired to have children at a particular time, as much as they tried, have been known to fail, only to conceive several months later when God is pleased to make the womb fruitful. So it is God who sovereignly bestows children as He wills. Why? Because they are His reward and He gives them to us. It is a *privilege* to receive children from God and he to whom God gives or grants the privilege of possessing children has a corresponding responsibility. In Ephesians 6 Paul lays upon parents, and especially upon fathers, the awesome responsibility of bringing up children in the nurture and admonition of the Lord, and a part of that nurture and admonition is found in Proverbs 23:13-14; "Do not hold back discipline from the child: although you beat him with the rod, he will not die. You shall beat him with the rod, and deliver his soul from Sheol."

It is natural for us to seek to withhold discipline from our children. It is much easier for us *to do something else or to be some place else,* but God requires of Christian parents and especially of Christian fathers that they administer the discipline which He reveals in His Word. For parents, and especially for fathers, to withhold that discipline is to sin against God and it is also to sin against the children that we say we love. To withhold that necessary correction is to rebel against the Lord. We must not avoid our responsibility, but rather we must seek God for grace to fulfill that responsibility which He has placed upon us. It is not a light thing, because the very souls of our children are the issues at hand. By administering discipline God says we will deliver their souls from hell. But if we withhold that discipline, we are responsible for the destruction of the souls of our own children!

Fourthly, the love which we as parents have toward our children demands that we correct them. It is natural to be tender and affectionate toward our own flesh and blood, but this tenderness and affection must not be used as an excuse to escape our responsibility. If we truly understand that our children are depraved and full of sin and are headed toward hell, and if we fully appreciate the responsibility which God has placed upon us as Christian parents, then genuine love must constrain us to discipline our children.

Our God commands us: "Chasten thy son while there is hope, and let not thy soul spare for his crying" (Prov. 19:18 AV). Discipline your son while there is hope. As long as you have any kind of control over him, as long as he is under your roof, and even beyond, you are to correct him. Eli was held responsible even though his sons had moved out of his tent and may have had their own wives and children. Eli was responsible to correct *his* children and as long as *our* children are alive there is hope that they may repent, believe on the Lord Jesus Christ, and be saved. As long as there is that hope and as long as they are alive it is our responsibility as Christian parents to offer them guidance, discipline, and correction. "Chasten thy son while there is hope, and let not thy soul spare for his crying." It hurts to hear your child cry and to know that you are the cause of that pain, but it hurts even more to realize that if they don't cry now, they will weep eternally and bitterly in the pain and anguish of hell. Better a little crying now than weeping and wailing and gnashing of teeth for eternity. Better to discipline them now while there is hope than to look back with hindsight after the day of judgment and say, "That's what I *should* have done; perhaps they could have been spared from eternal torment."

The Bible says in Proverbs 13:24, "He who spares his rod hates his son." "No," you say, "no, that's not true. I love my son. That's why I don't spank him. That's why I don't apply the rod to him." It is in reality because you despise him; it is because you think lightly of the eternal state of his soul. However you may convince yourself, God says the truth is otherwise and that the father who loves his child will chasten him betimes or early. He will chasten him early. Yes, when that babe just *begins* to manifest his rebellion against God and man, the father who loves his child will begin to chasten him. If you love your children, remember that *discipline is not hate; discipline is love*. We want our children to obey us because we love them. We want them to be good children because we love them. We want them to obey God because we love them and we want to see them saved and brought to a knowledge of the living God. That is why we apply the rod. If you apply the rod for any other reason, it is not biblical discipline. Biblical love demands the application of the rod.

The Bible gives us a number of examples of parents who allowed their emotions to control them. These were parents who allowed their tenderness and their affection to blind them with respect to their responsibilities. Bishop Ryle in his treatise on *The Duties of Parents* refers to two of these examples:

> Fathers and mothers, I tell you plainly, if you never punish your children when they are in fault, you are doing them a grievous wrong. I warn you, this is the rock on which the saints of God, in every age, have only too frequently made shipwreck. I would fain persuade you to be wise in time, and keep clear of it. See it in Eli's case. His sons Hophni and Phinehas "made themselves vile, and he restrained them not." He gave them no more than a tame and lukewarm reproof, when he ought to have rebuked them sharply. In one word, he honored his sons above God. And what was the end of these things? He lived to hear of the death of both his sons in battle, and his own grey hairs were brought down with sorrow to the grave.
>
> See, too, the case of David. Who can read without pain the history of his children, and their sins? Amnon's incest, Absalom's murder and proud rebellion, Adonijah's scheming ambition: truly these were grievous wounds for the man after God's own heart to receive from his own house. But was there no fault on his side? I fear there can be no doubt that there was. I find a clue to it all in the account

of Adonijah in 1 Kings 1:6 (AV): "His father had not displeased him at any time in saying, Why hast thou done so?" There was the foundation of all the mischief. David was an overindulgent father, a father who let his children have their own way, and he reaped according as he had sown.

These things in the Old Testament are recorded for our learning. We are to look at these examples in order to benefit from the experiences of Eli and of King David. They are not written as choice bits of gossip about the household of David; they are not written to cast doubt as to the spirituality of David; they are written that you and I may not follow in his footsteps. They are written that we may take heed and do all that God commands in every area of our lives, including the discipline of our children, lest our hearts be grieved within us at the end of our children. Oh, if you have children and if you love them, then see what God commands; see what God says must be true of a Christian parent. See the necessity of obeying God for the good of the child and for the glory of God Himself. "Withhold not correction from the child: for if thou beatest him with the rod, he shall not die. Thou shalt beat him with the rod, and shalt deliver his soul from hell." The application of discipline is an unmistakable requirement for all parents who would obey God.

REVIEW

1. What did John Locke say about the nature of a child?
2. What does *God* say about the child's nature?
3. If man was created in righteousness, why do children need to be corrected? What happened?
4. How has the Fall affected the image of God in man?
5. When are children responsible as sinners?
6. Who does God expect to train and discipline children?
7. Are love and correction opposed to one another?

RESPONSE

1. Since children are a gift from God, how can I demonstrate my gratitude?
2. How will this chapter help me to pray for (your child's name) ?
3. What is one important way for me to show my children that I love them?

3

The Biblical Motives
for Correction

In the last chapter we sought to show that it is necessary for us to correct our children. Scripture tells us that children *need* guidance and correction, and it is primarily the responsibility of parents to provide the required discipline. It is not the responsibility of the school, or of the church, or of the Boy Scouts, or of any other organization to replace parents in this very important realm. God has placed this responsibility upon parents, and they alone can provide the proper correction.

In this chapter we want to consider the biblical motives for correction. So we must ask ourselves questions such as these: What are the scriptural motives for disciplining our children? What reasons do we have for administering the rod? What do we hope to accomplish by means of correction?

The text which provides the title for this study provides us with an immediate motive, and a very important one: "Withhold not correction from the child: for if thou beatest him with the rod, he shall not die. Thou shalt beat him with the rod, and shalt deliver his soul from hell" (Prov. 23:13-14 AV).

Now admittedly this motive is set in something of a negative context. We are to beat the child with a rod in order to spare him from something worse: to deliver his soul from hell. Later on we'll look at a more positive approach toward the motive for discipline, but I think it is right and necessary for us to begin with this immediate motive.

Some time ago, when my oldest child, Nathan, was just learning how to go up and down the slides in a local park, he managed one day to climb all the way to the top of the tallest slide. He ascended to the top step by step, but as he got to the top rung he let go of the railings and fell backward. He caught me somewhat offguard—I was standing behind him, but I wasn't expecting him to fall. I instinctively reached out my arms to catch him; to break his fall in order to keep him from bashing his brains against that bottom step. I wasn't especially concerned at that point about a positive approach to his education; I was more concerned that he not receive a negative or even a *disastrous* educational experience. I *had* to break his fall. I had to catch him. I had to change his downward plummet.

Parents, our children are falling! It is not the ground at the bottom of the slide that waits for them, but their descent is toward hell. They are falling, and our intuitive reaction ought to be to reach out to catch them, to break their fall, and to change their direction. We must stop them from their downward descent before we can instill in them the positive principles that will enable them to climb upward once again. It is in the light of this truth that we are to administer discipline, for Solomon says, "You shall beat him with the rod, and deliver his soul from Sheol." The discipline of the home is that force which can change the direction of the child or at least retard the breakneck speed with which he makes his steady descent. It is in the realization of this fact that Solomon can say to us, "Chasten thy son while there is hope, and let not thy soul spare for his crying" (Prov. 19:18 AV). Oh, it hurts a parent to administer discipline and the child cries when discipline is properly administered, but Solomon says to shut your ears against it. Do not let the crying of the child sway you from your God-given responsibility to discipline him. Realize what you are doing when you apply the rod. It may have hurt Nathan when I caught him around the ribs or if I caught him around the neck, but he was caught and whether it hurt him or not, it spared him from a greater disaster. Do not let the crying of the child sway you from administering discipline because you are sparing him from a *greater* disaster by administering the rod—it may be that you shall deliver his soul from hell.

This motive for biblical discipline springs from the love which God has given parents for their children. God has given us a natural affection and tenderness toward our own offspring. When Nathan was only two months old he required surgery. We brought him into the hospital and left him there under the constant care and attention of various doctors and nurses. Some tell us that at this age a child is not really aware of *who* is loving him so long as *someone* is loving him. Nevertheless, when we put our first-born into the hospital we came to visit him every day and stood outside the nursery watching through the window. Each time I saw one of the nurses come to take a blood sample (in an infant they lance the baby's heel in order to extract blood) I wanted to take Nathan outside and let the nurse cut my heel in his place. God has given us a natural affection and tenderness toward our own offspring. I am certain that all who are parents have experienced that same feeling. When your children have a high temperature or when they have a terribly uncomfortable disease, you wish that you could suffer in their place and bear their infirmities.

This is not at all uncommon; the Apostle Paul had that same feeling toward some people that he loved. They were not his natural children and yet they were people whom he loved very much. He tells us of this affection in the ninth chapter of his letter to the Romans. He says, "I am telling the truth in Christ, I am not lying, my conscience bearing me witness in the Holy Spirit, that I have great sorrow and unceasing grief in my heart. For I could wish that I myself were accursed, separated from Christ for the sake of my brethren, my kinsmen according to the flesh" (Rom. 9:1-3). Paul is telling us here that as he looks out upon his kinsmen according to the flesh, those who are Jews, he has such an overwhelming love for them that he wishes he could be sent to hell in their place that they might be spared. How great a love this is! It is like unto the love of the parent for a child to wish that we could endure all affliction, all pain, all sorrow, yea, even to wish that we could endure the pains of eternal hell if only our children might be spared. But this is not possible. It was not possible for the Apostle Paul, and therefore, in order to see his kinsmen spared from hell, Paul must go to them and preach unto them the Gospel which alone can deliver them from hell. If we would see our children spared, we must go to them and in love administer biblical discipline. We cannot take their place. Therefore we must do everything in our power to deliver them from hell by administering biblical discipline.

However, there is also a more positive motive for discipline. Paul tells us about this in Ephesians 6:4: "And, fathers, do not provoke your children to anger; but bring them up in the discipline and instruction of the Lord." In this verse Paul sets forth the positive motive for administering biblical discipline. All parental acts of guidance and discipline must be governed by the teaching of this text. This text is definitive of biblical discipline, and if we administer the rod without taking into account what Paul says here, we are falling short of *biblical* discipline. All discipline, all guidance, and we may even expand that to say all education, must be viewed in the light of Ephesians 6:4.

Paul begins by telling fathers what is *not* a proper motive for discipline. Frequently in the Scriptures we find the positive set against the negative. In 1 Corinthians, for example, the Apostle Paul tells us that women are to be silent in the church, and lest we misunderstand that he tells us that what he means is that they are not to speak in the church. Here in Ephesians 6 Paul addresses himself to fathers and he says that we are to bring up our children in the discipline and instruction of the Lord. What he means is that that we are not to provoke our children to wrath. Fathers are not to create in their children feelings of anger or frustration caused by undue severity, by injustice in the application of discipline, or by an inconsistent or an unreasonable exercise of authority. Discipline is not an opportunity for parents, especially fathers, to build up their own egos at the expense of their children. The administration of discipline is not an opportunity for us to air our wrath or to vent our own personal frustrations at the expense of our little ones.

Neither is it an opportunity for us to exercise authority in the absolute sense as though we were tyrants. Some fathers are at the bottom of the totem pole at work, and yet in their hearts they desire to rule and reign. When they come home after 5:00, they act like the boss, sitting in their easy chairs issuing commands back and forth. Everyone had better hop to it and obey or the ax will fall. That is the attitude of the dictator, not of the father who loves his family and who administers biblical discipline only because he *does love* his children.

Rather, the responsibility of godly parents is to "bring them up in the discipline and instruction of the Lord." What does that mean? "Bring them up. . . ." This is our responsibility, and we had better know what Paul means when he says to bring them up in the nurture and admonition of the Lord.

This word *discipline* or *nurture* is a rather comprehensive term, and it refers to the whole process of educating the child. It is translated *discipline* here in Ephesians 6, *training* in 2 Timothy 3, and *chastening* or *chastisement* in Hebrews 12 (AV). Thus it refers to the whole process of education. Nurture involves instruction and chastisement or discipline. All who are engaged at any point in the educational process of children are responsible to bring them up in accordance with the instruction and discipline of the Lord. This includes pastors, teachers, babysitters, grandmothers and grandfathers, aunts and uncles, but especially parents. To bring them up in the discipline of the Lord is to bring them up in the instruction and in the chastening which is prescribed by Him. This means much more than simply sending our children to Sunday School, even more than sending them to Sunday School and church. To bring them up in the nurture and admonition of the Lord means that we are responsible to bring them up in a context which is governed totally by scriptural precepts and principles. This truth has tremendous implications with respect to the establishment of schools that are truly Christian, but here we are primarily concerned with the family situation so I am going to pass up that temptation and stick to our immediate area of concern.

Deuteronomy 6 gives us a good picture of the biblical family. Deuteromy 6:4-9 says, "Hear, O Israel! The Lord is our God, the Lord is one! And you shall love the Lord your God with all your heart and with all your soul and with all your might. And these words, which I am commanding you

today, shall be on your heart; and you shall teach them diligently to your sons and shall talk of them when you sit in
your house and when you walk by the way and when you
lie down and when you rise up. And you shall bind them as
a sign on your hand and they shall be as frontals on your
forehead. And you shall write them on the doorposts of your
house and on your gates." This passage gives us a glimpse of
the ideal family, that is, the family which is totally governed
in its context by scriptural principles and precepts. Look at
what the parents are doing. In verse 7 "you shall teach them
[your children] diligently." We are to teach the words which
God has delivered to our children, and to talk of them whenever we sit in our houses, and when we walk by the way, and
when we lie down, and when we rise up. This is not a picture
of a ritualistic home. This is a picture of a home which has
both formal instruction and informal instruction in the Word
of God. It is natural in the family context to talk about spiritual matters. This doesn't mean that we always have our
Bibles open, teaching our children out of this Book. Our
children may come to us with a question: "Sammy says that
he is going to go over to Farmer Jones' property to pick
some apples off his trees. Can I go?" It doesn't mean necessarily that we have to open the Bible and preach to him for
half an hour before our child understands. It means simply
that we talk to him and explain to him what the Bible has to
say about matters such as this.

A man said to me recently (and this objection comes fairly
frequently), "I can't spend all of my time praying, reading
the Bible, and teaching my children diligently. I have a business to operate; I have shutters to nail; I have rooms that
need to be painted. I just cannot live this Christian life as you
define it." Look at the parents here. Verse 6, "these words,
which I am commanding you today, shall be on your heart."
The parents who fulfill the biblical injunction have the truth

in their hearts. It is easy enough to show that this means the truth has become a vital part of them. They have received biblical precepts to such an extent that it is natural for them to order their lives according to the Scriptures, and therefore it is natural for them to give guidance and direction to their children according to scriptural precepts. A man must be converted himself before he can teach others about the responsibilities that God has laid before him. The Bible says that a man who is in Christ is a new creature and it will be natural for him to instruct others in the way of God. It is said of John Bunyan that if you pricked him any place his blood would flow Bibline. That ought not to be true simply of Bunyan or of other extraordinarily powerful preachers of the Word. That ought to be true of every one of us who names the name of Christ. If we were to be cut any place, if our hearts were to be laid bare before the world, our insides would be seen to be Bibline: so governed by the Word of God that it is natural for us to instruct our children according to biblical principle.

What is the purpose of instructing our children? "These words . . . shall be on your heart; and you shall teach them diligently." What words? The words which precede, obviously, in verses 4 and 5: "Hear, O Israel! The Lord is our God, the Lord is one! And you shall love the Lord your God with all your heart and with all your soul and with all your might." All the instruction which we give to our children, all the guidance and direction which we as parents or as teachers give to our children is to the end that they may love the Lord their God!

That brings us to the second word in Ephesians 6: "Do not provoke your children to anger; but bring them up in the discipline and instruction of the Lord." The word *instruction* or *admonition* here in Ephesians 6 is a combination of two Greek words which mean "to put or to place in mind." It is

translated in the Scriptures as *admonition, admonish,* and
warn. Charles Hodge, who was professor of Systematic The-
ology at Princeton Seminary some years ago, says that "it is
the act of *reminding* one of his faults or duties." Notice this:
we are to bring up our children in the admonition *of the
Lord!* We are not *simply* to remind our children of their
faults or duties. We are not simply to admonish them; that is
nagging. To constantly be laying before your children their
faults and saying, "you dum-dum, you can't do anything
right, can you?"—that is not biblical admonition. That is sinful nagging. Biblical admonition is to warn them, to admonish
them, to bring them up in the admonition *of the Lord.* This
means that when we remind our children of their faults and
of their duties, we must admonish them in the context of
their responsibility to God. We must not simply tell them
that they have failed; but we must remind them that they
have failed in their obligations to God.

This is the grand motive for all of our discipline and all of
our instruction from the earliest months to the later years.
Our motive for discipline is to bring our children into a subordinate relationship to the authority of the living God and
not just to ourselves. If we seek to make our children submit
to us alone, we have failed in our biblical responsibility.
Rather, God says that we are to bring them into submission
to Him. All of our discipline, nurture, instruction, and warn-
ings must be framed in this context: To bring them to the
point where they become obedient disciples of Jesus Christ.
So you see the motive for biblical doctrine is not just to
rescue our children from hell (although that is part of it), but
more importantly, it is to bring them into life in Jesus
Christ.

See how this works out practically. Paul, when he admonishes children in this very context, says what? "Children,
obey your parents because I tell you to. . ."? *That is not*

what he says. "Children, obey your parents in the Lord, for this is right. Honor your father and mother (which is the first commandment with a promise), that it may be well with you, and that you may live long on the earth" (Eph. 6: 2-3). When Paul admonishes children he relates them to the authority of God expressed through His commandment. He does not say, "Obey your parents because I tell you to." He says, "Obey your parents because God has given an express commandment demanding this. You are responsible before God to obey your parents." Charles Hodge says that God's authority "should be brought into constant and immediate contact with the mind, heart, and conscience of the child." This means that we as parents must not set ourselves up as the ultimate source of knowledge and as the possessors of authority to determine truth and duty. Any authority that we have as parents is a delegated authority. We must realize this. God has given us children and he has delegated authority to exercise rule over our children; but the authority that we have is only delegated to us by Jesus Christ, who possesses all authority in heaven and on earth. In a very practical way we must learn to encourage obedience in our children, not demanding "do it because I said to," but "do this because God says 'obey your parents in the Lord.' Do this because God says you ought to do it and you are responsible to Him." We must always seek to relate our children to the authority of God Himself. In what is sometimes known as *Authoritarian Ethics,* it is *God* who is the Authority behind the Ethics! We need to remember that.

In summary, then, as we administer discipline it is on the one hand to stop the present direction of our children. Nothing less than the administration of the rod can have that effect. Secondly, and greater, the grand motive for all of our discipline is to bring our children into a subordinate, submissive relationship to the authority of God Himself.

But before we can do that we, ourselves, must be under the authority of God. Do you know Jesus Christ? You cannot train your children unless you know Him. You cannot possibly raise your children in a way that will be honoring to God unless you, yourself, first of all know Jesus Christ. Do you know Him? Have you repented of sin? Have you believed on Him? Are you seeking to obey Him? Then proceed to administer discipline in order that you may bring your children into the same relationship to God that you have. If you do not have that relationship, you must immediately repent. God commands all men everywhere to repent and that command is issued to every one of you who have read this far. Do not proceed to chapter four until your heart is right before God. Turn from your wickedness and live. Right now there is only one word for you: repent, repent, repent.

REVIEW

1. What are the scriptural motives for disciplining our children?
   Immediate?
   Long-range?
2. What is the *discipline* of the Lord?
3. What is meant by *admonition?*

RESPONSE

1. In the light of scriptural teaching, is it important *to me* to learn how to discipline my children biblically?
2. Is my family like the family in Deuteronomy 6? Why, or why not?
3. What things can I do to practically relate my children to the authority of God?
4. Do I know Jesus Christ well enough to introduce my children to Him?

4

God's Authority in Discipline

In the last chapter we concluded that the motive for all correction from birth until the adult years is to bring our children into a subordinate relationship to the living God. In other words, and more simply expressed, the object of all correction according to the Bible is to help our children to become obedient disciples of our Lord Jesus Christ. All parental acts of guidance, discipline, and correction must be governed by this supreme motive which bears tremendously important implications with respect to the method of the application of correction.

How are we to administer correction in our homes? The *first* implication of the fact that we are to bring up our children in the nurture and admonition of the Lord is this: We must discipline our children under God's authority. This means several things. To discipline or correct our children under the authority of God means in the first instance that I, as a parent, must continually remind myself that any authority that I may possess is an authority which is delegated to me by the good pleasure of God. Any authority which I have is not by right; I possess authority as a parent only because God has delegated it to me. There is a little bit of the tyrant in every one of us. Some men have an opportunity to express this desire to exercise sovereignty in their occupation. Perhaps they own their own company or manage a particular division of a company. They may have only one or two men working beneath them, but their business provides sufficient opportunity to exercise this sovereignty. There are other men who do not have that opportunity. They are not at the top of the line so far as their company is concerned; they are at the bottom and the only thing that they exercise sovereignty over is the broom. They then seek to exercise this tyranny in the home, and they rule their wives and children with an iron hand. They enter their homes and their wives and children fear them. When they speak, their families jump at every command. Women, too, are not immune to this desire to be a tyrant. Some women exercise this kind of control over their husbands. Other women exercise this kind of control over their children. They are at home with the children day after day, week after week. When they have an inconsiderate husband to whom they must render obedience, they sometimes take out their resentment against the children, exercising a tyranny over them. Children likewise have a desire to rule, and so we will see our children bossing the dog around, spanking the cat, yelling at the bird, and otherwise seeking to imitate mom and dad.

This is *not* the kind of authority that we can or ought to exercise. This is sinful. God alone has absolute and ultimate authority; any authority that I have as a parent is only delegated to me by Him. I am not a tyrant. I cannot function as a tyrant. I must realize that as a parent I am in a subordinate relationship to God and I only exercise the authority which He has given to me. I cannot establish what is right and what is wrong; I can only declare what *God* says is right and wrong in my home. I cannot establish what is true and what is false.

As a parent with an authority delegated to me by God I can only declare to my children what *God* says is true and what God says is false. Now this means a great deal when we begin to grasp this principle. It means that as a parent I must recognize that my authority does not depend upon my being older or bigger or smarter than my children. I know that some parents think that their authority *is* dependent upon that, and that when their children get so big that they can no longer spank them they will lose control over them. Or they think that when their children progress in high school or college to a level higher than the greatest achievement of their academic life, then they will lose control. After all, when children are bigger than you and smarter than you, how can you possibly exercise control over them? The unhappy result of such thinking is that some parents allow their children to run over them without restraints, and their homes are chaotic. Our authority as parents is *not* dependent upon our ability to put our children into submission either physically or mentally. We as parents and as teachers must realize that we exercise parental responsibility and authority because God has so ordained it by giving us children, and it is in obedience to Him that we are to apply the rod of correction. Our authority exists as long as we are parents to that child because God has ordained it. Our authority rests upon *God's* authority, not upon the shifting virtues of age, physical prowess, or mental ability. I as a parent must realize that I possess authority only because God has given it to me.

A *second* implication is that my children must be made aware of the ultimate and absolute authority of God as well. In the words of Charles Hodge, God's authority "should be brought into constant and immediate contact with the mind, heart, and conscience of the child." Not only must I as a parent be aware that my authority exists because God has given it to me, but I must labor to bring my children into constant and immediate contact with the authority of God. Very practically (and we want to be practical) we must encourage our children to obey, not merely "because I say so," but to obey because *God* says "Children, obey your parents in the Lord, for this is right" (Eph. 6:1).

This is not something that we can learn overnight. It is something that we need to *labor* with as parents and as teachers—how to bring the authority of God into direct and immediate contact with the child. Only when we do this has *biblical* discipline been administered. It is not biblical discipline to simply slap our child and say, "I don't want you to do that any more." It is only *biblical* discipline when we have labored to bring *God's authority* to bear upon him. It is a principle that must be worked out in the day-to-day life situations in which we find ourselves. It is a principle that can only be worked out as we grow with our child, being sensitive to his background in the Word of God, continually applying God's authority to him. For some of us it will be exceptionally difficult work; we will have to unlearn a lot of false precepts and concepts in order to apply the truth, but it is essential for the well-being of the child that the authority of God be clearly manifested in the exercise of parental discipline. It is essential for our children that we go through the pains and difficulties of making such an adjustment.

See how Paul reproves in Ephesians 6:1, "Children, obey your parents in the Lord, for this is right." Now how does Paul support that principle? He is talking to children here, isn't he? With what word does Paul begin? Is he addressing parents? No. Is he addressing preachers of the Word? No. Is he addressing Sunday School teachers? No. He is talking directly to children and he says, "Children, you little ones, you obey your parents in the Lord for this is right." Then he backs up the principle by bringing God's authority immediately to bear upon the child: "Honor your father and

mother (which is the first commandment with a promise),
that it may be well with you, and that you may live long on
the earth" (Eph. 6:2-3). Do you see, parents, how Paul corrects the children here? He addresses them: *Children;* he establishes the principle: *Obey your parents in the Lord, for
this is right;* then he directly applies *God's authority* by quot-
ing an Old Testament passage: *Honor your father and
mother, that it may be well with you, and that you may live
long on the earth.* He does not merely quote pious platitudes
to them; he also *explains* the passage in the parenthesis in
verse 2: "which is the first commandment with a promise."
He reminds them that the God who gave this commandment
has also issued a promise—that is the way that discipline
ought to be administered. This is how we ought to be correcting our children. See how Paul does it: he addresses them,
he establishes the principle, he supports the principle by directly applying the Word of God, and he explains the selected
passage from the Word of God.

Now honestly, how often do we take the time to correct
our children in this manner? How often do we really seek to
apply the Word of God to them in their particular violation
of the Law? How often in the context of administering the
rod do we apply verbal reproof in the form of bringing an
admonition from the Scriptures? We do err when we neglect
this. We disobey God and we treat our children unjustly
when we fail to administer biblical discipline. Oh, this is not
going to be easy to learn; this is hard. But it is essential for
the child that God's authority be constantly and immediately
applied to his day-to-day, moment-to-moment situation. We
must follow the example of the Apostle Paul in correcting
our children.

The book of Proverbs is especially valuable in bringing to
mind Scriptures to apply to specific situations. For example,
if your children are teasing one another and heading toward a

fight, don't just say: "All right, break it up; move aside—you sit here! You sit there!" Warn them, but warn them in the words of Proverbs 17:14, "The beginning of strife is like letting out water, so abandon the quarrel before it breaks out." Explain the text to your children. Remind them of the time that they built a little dam or dike out of mud. Help them to recall how they scraped their finger across the top and the water began to run over and before long all the mud had been worn away and there was a regular flood. Explain to them that this teasing, provoking, and agitating one another is like the hole that they made in that dike and the water is going to come pouring out and somebody is going to end up with a bloody nose if they don't watch it. Apply the Scriptures, the authority of God, in their immediate context.

If your children are restless, fussy, and they've got ants in their pants in the middle of the worship service or some place else where you want them to sit quietly, don't just hit them on the side of the leg and say, "Be quiet! Sit still!" Why not open your Bible to Proverbs 25:28 (AV) and apply the authority of God to them where the Lord declares, "He that hath no rule over his own spirit is like a city that is broken down, and without walls." What is the significance of a city that is broken down and without walls? All the strong cities of biblical days were walled cities, and a city that had lost its walls had lost its defense. Anyone or anything could trample right over it. Explain to your children that if they cannot control their own spirits, if they cannot control themselves, they're ripe for anything, or anyone to come along and lead them astray. Warn them that it is necessary for them to discipline their bodies in order to maintain control over their spirits. Having explained that to them it would be very simple in the midst of a service to simply open your Bible to Proverbs 25 and point your finger to verse 28. A light will flick on in their minds saying, "Yes, God says I had better control myself. I had better straighten up."

Perhaps you are having a difficult time with your children always telling tales that are sometimes true and sometimes not. "Mommy, Johnny hit me." "Mommy, Johnny's not sitting on the step where he's supposed to be—he moved up one," and all the rest. What do you do in this situation? Well, possibly you could turn to Proverbs 17 again and remind them of verse 9 where God says, "He who covers a transgression seeks love, but he who repeats a matter separates intimate friends." "Listen, Susan, do you want Johnny to be your friend? This is not the way to do it." "Listen, Billy, Johnny is your brother and you have to live with him. You had better realize right now that 'he who covers a transgression seeks love, but he who repeats a matter separates intimate friends.' You're not going to get along if you continue to be a tattletale—God says so. God tells us how to have friends, and this is not the way." Maybe you would want to look at Proverbs 18:8 (AV) "The words of a talebearer are as wounds, and they go down into the innermost parts of the belly." Remind your child of the great harm, the great pain and anguish that he is causing Johnny when he always comes running to tell everything that Johnny did and even adds to the story, making it worse than it really was. Or you could turn to Proverbs 26. (See what I mean about Proverbs being exceptionally valuable?) Proverbs are intended to be memorized. These are verses that we can memorize with our children and then when we are in an appropriate situation we can apply God's authority by beginning to quote the verse and allowing them to finish it and explain it. Proverbs 26:20 (AV) says, "Where no wood is, there the fire goeth out: so where there is no talebearer, the strife ceaseth." "Ah, Susan, you say you don't get along with Johnny. Johnny doesn't like you. Maybe if you wouldn't keep telling your mother everything that Johnny does you would get along better. Where there's no wood there's no fire; where there's no talebearer the strife ceases. You have so few friends because you are a tattletale, and God says that if you want friends you must conduct yourself differently."

Perhaps your son has been called an unpleasant name by another child, and he begins to respond in like manner. Maybe he reacts violently—even punching the other boy in the nose! A word is sufficient; indeed only a *turn* of a word is sufficient to cause violence between children and even between men. Direct your child to Proverbs 15:1, "A gentle answer turns away wrath, but a harsh word stirs up anger." "When somebody calls you a nasty name and you call him another name back, he's going to call you another name and then you're going to call him another name, and anger is going to be stirred up and it's going to come to blows—but, Johnny, when you respond to that nasty name with a gentle answer you just wipe him out. He doesn't know how to respond. He doesn't know how to come back at you and you've stopped effectively what might have been a disastrous situation, because, after all, Billy's bigger than you are. You've exercised control over the situation; you've responded in the way that God says: 'with a gentle answer.'"

It may be that your child wants to open up his lemonade stand on the Lord's Day and you feel certain that the Christian Sabbath is not a time for that type of activity. Instead of saying, "Get in the house. I'm not going to let you do this—no, no, no," why not simply direct him to Proverbs 16:16 and show your child how much better it is to get wisdom than gold and that to get understanding is rather to be chosen than silver. Why not direct your child to this passage and show him that it is much greater on the Lord's Day to come into the home to have family devotions, to pray together, to read the Scriptures, and to make it a family day than to sell lemonade for a nickel a glass. Open the Scriptures with him. Teach him some songs. See to it that he has an abundant wealth of literature available to him so that if he wants to have some time alone he can go aside and read. Show him and instill in him this attitude: That it is *better to do this* than to be outside selling lemonade on the Lord's Day. Isn't that much better, and isn't that directly applying God's authority to his problem area?

If your children blaspheme or if they lie, take them to Exodus 20 and explain God's Law to them, showing them examples in Scripture of how God deals with violators. Yes, let them see it. Let them see that God killed people in the Old Testament for the very thing that Johnny did this afternoon. Let them see that if a man blasphemed in the Old Testament he was to be taken outside the camp and stoned; if a child cursed his mother or spoke out against his father and manifested a rebellious spirit that could not seem to be brought under control, that child was to be taken outside the camp and stoned. Let your children see that *God is displeased,* not just that you are. Apply *God's* authority and let them see that God is displeased with this type of activity.

Then, after having explained the Law, showing them examples of how God dealt with that in the Old Testament and warning them that continuing in that type of activity will drive them to hell, reinforce the lesson by the administration of the rod. Correction is not complete until you have done that. Impress it upon their minds, which in children sometimes seems to be located in the seat, so that they understand that God does not like this kind of behavior and that each time they manifest that wicked, perverse nature they must be corrected because God has demanded it.

If, in the particular area in which your child is disobedient, you cannot think of any specific text, then take him back to Ephesians 6 and impress upon him even as Paul did,

"Children, obey your parents in the Lord, for this is right."
Ephesians 6:1 can be a kind of sanctified *catch-all*. If you are
unable to think of a specific text to cover your peculiar situation, come to this one but do not just say, "I don't want you
to do it because I don't want you to do it." You are *still* responsible to apply the authority of God and you can effectively do this by directing your child to Ephesians 6:1.
"Johnny, I want you to obey me because God says, 'Children
obey your parents in the Lord, for this is right.'" It is just as
easy and more correct to say, "Do it because *God says so*,"
than to say, "Do it because *I say so.*" By directing your child
to Ephesians 6, you are bringing him into immediate contact
with God's authority and if I am to discipline my children
then they must realize that it is God whom they have offended. It is God with whom they have to deal. I as a parent
and teacher administer discipline only as an ambassador, as a
representative of God.

Thirdly, to bring up my children under God's authority
means that parental guidance and correction is intended to
be a reflection of God's dealings with his spiritual offspring.
Not only should the child see the authority of God *behind*
the authority of the parent, but the child should also see the
manner and attitude of God reflected *in* the parent as he administers discipline and correction in His name. God's good-
ness, God's justice, God's mercy, God's loving concern, and
God's care for his people should all be identifiable in the
parent's approach to discipline. In effect, through administering biblical correction the parent is preaching a sermon
to his child. He is preaching a sermon which reveals something of the nature of God, something of the nature of man
(specifically of the child), something of the character and nature of sin, and also something of the judgment or the consequences of that sin. This is what makes biblical discipline
distinctively a religious action. In fact, we may even go so far

as to say that biblical discipline is an act of divine worship. How so? It is glorifying God through obedience to Him; it is revealing, instructing, and manifesting something of the character and nature of God to the child.

Fathers, do you realize that when you administer discipline it is an act of worship? Do you approach discipline with that in mind? Are you concerned to accurately portray the character of God as you wield that rod? Do you keep in mind your supreme motive, which is to bring your child into a subordinate relationship to the authority of God? Fathers, you are to be a reflection of our Lord Jesus Christ in the home. As Christ is the Head of the Church, so you are to be head in your home.

You are to be prophets in your homes. Are you teaching your children? Are you teaching them through spankings, through the administration of the rod, through discipline? Do you accompany that discipline with the Word or do you slap them, hit them, or maybe even kick them, and that's it? Is your discipline administered in a context of worship or is it done out of anger and frustration? Do you reflect accurately the tender mercies of God who when He chastises His children does so as an act of love, or do you beat them and leave them so that they think if you're an example of what God is like, God must be a harsh, nasty individual. Oh, this is important.

Fathers, you are to be priests in your home; you are to intercede for your children. When you spank them, do you intercede for them? When you get up in the morning, do you earnestly pray that your children may understand the Word of God this day and obey it? Do you pray that as you administer discipline they may be brought into union with Jesus Christ?

Fathers, you are to be kings in your homes; you are to take the authority in the home, but not a tyrannical authority.

God has appointed you king in your home and you are to exercise that kingship. Do you leave all matters of discipline to your wife, who spends more time with the children, or do you take upon yourself the responsibilities which God has laid upon you? It is very tempting, isn't it, to shift the responsibility for correction onto another. Mothers are tempted to say, "Wait until daddy gets home," and daddy becomes the bad guy. Daddy is very tempted sometimes to say, "Wife, why don't you put a stop to this? Why don't you do something about it? You're around them more than I am, you do it. I don't want to give my children a bad image so that every time I'm around them they think I'm going to spank them." So daddy never administers the rod. That's wrong, too. Husband, you are to be king and any authority to administer discipline that your wife has is delegated to her by you in your absence; but when you are there and when you are aware of what is going on, it is your responsibility to administer discipline, reflecting the manner and the attitude of God.

This realm of correction is truly holy ground. The more I read in the Scriptures about it the more I realize how frequently I have made mistakes in the past and the more I realize how holy a function discipline really is. If we are to accurately reflect the character of God in the way in which we discipline our children, we had better *know* the character of God. We had better be certain before we ever try to implement biblical discipline that we, ourselves, are under God's authority. We had better make our own calling and election sure; we had better ask ourselves, "Have I been genuinely converted; have I been born anew from above by the Spirit of God? Have I repented of sin? Have I turned from sin to serve the true and the living God? Do I own Jesus Christ to be my prophet, my priest, and my king?" Is this the standard by which you seek to operate and to live out your life? We can never, never, never properly administer biblical discipline in our homes until we, ourselves, are brought under God's authority, have laid down our weapons of warfare, and have ceased in our strife and rebellion against God. The Bible declares that all the world is guilty before Him. The Bible declares that there is not one righteous, no, not one on all the face of the earth. Among all the teeming millions of people there is not one righteous individual by nature. There is none that understands; there is none that seeks after God. The Bible says that all have sinned and it says that the wages of sin is death. The Bible says that by nature we are dead on account of trespasses and sins. The Bible says that we are children who deserve only the wrath and the curse of God.

Whether you be mother, father, or teacher, apart from Jesus Christ you are caught up in the swirling waters which descend into hell. You cannot save any child's soul from going to hell by administering biblical discipline so long as you are moving in that same direction. Think of it. How can you bring another one to safety if you, yourself, are drowning? How can you bring another out of the fire if you, yourself, are burning? How can you bring a child under the authority of God when you, yourself, are in rebellion against Him? Lay hold on Jesus Christ. Whoever you are, lay hold on Him "whom God displayed publicly as a propitiation in His blood through faith. . ." (Rom. 3:25), and the Bible declares that Jesus Christ is the only mediator between God and men. No other man, no angels, no saint, no church, and no organization can secure forgiveness for you before God. Jesus Christ is the way, the truth, and the life. Only they who come unto Him, who bow the knee before Him and acknowledge Him to be sovereign Lord and redeemer, who learn to rely and trust only upon His shed blood poured out on Calvary's tree to be a sacrifice for sin, shall be saved. And only these mothers, fathers, and teachers or preachers can be the means by which children shall be brought under the authority of God. Oh, may God grant to everyone reading these pages grace to bow before Jesus Christ, grace to acknowledge Him as having sovereignty, right, and kingship over us. May God grant that every one of us may be brought into obedience for His sake, and not only for His sake, but for the sake of all the children committed to our care.

REVIEW

1. What is the source of my authority as a parent?
2. How did the Apostle Paul reprove children?
3. In what sense can discipline be said to be an act of worship?

RESPONSE

1. Have I consciously brought the authority of God to bear upon my children?
2. Do I act as though *I* am the ultimate authority, or am I conscious of my role under God?
3. If I am a father, have I accepted my position and responsibility in the home?
4. If I am a mother, how do I help my husband to be prophet, priest, and king?

5

The Place of Prayer

What does prayer have to do with disciplining children? *Everything*—if we really meant what we said in the last chapter. As we live under God's authority we function as *stewards*. A steward is a manager. He doesn't really *own* anything, but he serves the true owner by managing his affairs: handling his finances, caring for his property, and supervising his other servants or employees. The owner must *trust* his manager, and the manager must demonstrate that he is *responsible*. God has entrusted us with the fruit of the womb—nothing in all of creation is more valuable. The Lord opens the womb and gives a child—perhaps several—to a man and his wife to manage and to raise to maturity. This is a stewardship. Though our children are flesh of our flesh, we don't own them. They're not ours. We are responsible to manage them for Another who has made them for Himself.

This is a very great responsibility: the greatest. If we manage a business and we fail, it will mean economic embarrassment and some temporary hardships. But if we manage a child and we fail, misery will follow for generations to come. Are we sufficient for such a task?

What do we do when we run into difficulties? The manager consults with the owner. For us as Christian parents, that means prayer. We need to have frequent and regular conferences with the Owner under whose name we labor. Prayer follows upon God's authority, and is absolutely essential to biblical discipline.

The Owner has not only told us *what* we must do, He has also told us in His Word *how* we must do it! We are to manage the children committed to our care by bringing them up in the discipline and instruction (nurture and admonition) *of the Lord!* Well! At least *that's* settled! We don't have to sort through all the paperbacks representing all the ideas and opinions of men in order to do our job as stewards under God. What we *do* need to do is to discover His will for us as parents as it is revealed in His written revelation, the Bible.

The Scriptures (as we shall soon see) set some very high standards and expectations for parents who are serious about being responsible stewards in the area of administering discipline. Many of us will have a great deal of re-thinking and reforming to do in order to bring our methods into submission to what the Word of God teaches.

We need to pray—first of all—for ourselves. Not one of us can obey the Scriptures in *any* area of life apart from the continuing grace of our Lord Jesus Christ. We cannot meet the requirements of God in the strength of our own flesh. We need to pray earnestly that our God would work in us to change us so that we can begin to implement truly biblical correction in our homes. When we lack wisdom, or lack the will to do as *Wisdom* directs, we need to remember that He "is able to do exceeding abundantly beyond all that we ask or think, according to the power that works within us" (Eph. 3:20). This gives us hope (confidence) as parents that though our task is great, our God is even greater! His grace will indeed prove to be sufficient for our needs.

Then we need to pray for our children. Remember that our motive in discipline is to deliver their souls from hell and to relate them subordinately to the authority of God. In other words, what we hope to accomplish is to restrain them from sin and to bring them to salvation. In this light biblical correction can be understood as a means of grace, or a channel by which children can be brought into a living relationship with the Lord.

Solomon tells us of two other channels used by God to bring men to faith: the Word of God and fervent, effectual prayer. Proverbs 2 is a wonderful chapter for showing the relationship between human responsibility and divine sovereignty. Receiving the Word and praying are distinctly human activities (vss. 1-5). But they will accomplish nothing unless they are accompanied by a corresponding act of divine sovereignty (vss. 6-9). Men can know God by means of the Word and prayer *only* because "the Lord gives wisdom." Neither reading the Bible nor praying will bring a man to salvation unless God is pleased to do a mighty work of grace within his heart. So it is with our children. We can administer the rod under God's authority with all firmness, and with all persevering consistency in a context of love, and it will come to nothing unless God works a work of grace in their hearts. We need to pray for our children. Pray that the Lord would use discipline as a means, accompanying that act of human responsibility with grace unto salvation. Pray that your children may be born again, quickened unto life by the Spirit of all grace. Ask God to grant them repentance and faith, lest all of your disciplinary efforts be in vain. We can never assume that if we properly raise our children they will automatically be Christians. There are too many examples in the Scriptures of godly parents who had wicked offspring. Spurgeon once said, "An honored father may have disgraceful sons." We need to pray for our children to know the Lord.

And we need to pray with our children. Biblical correction must be accompanied by earnest prayer. Our objective is to confront our children with the real authority of the living God. They need to see that when they disobey they have not only offended *us*. More seriously, they have offended *the Lord*. Therefore when they acknowledge their sins and ask forgiveness, they need to bring their confession and petition to Him. The child needs not only to be assured of the love that *you* have for him, but he must also be assured of the love that *God* has for him. That assurance flows in the context of prayer and can only come from the Lord Himself. Therefore, whenever possible, be sure to accompany the administration of the rod with prayer. Be sure to pray *with* your child.

This chapter may be short, but don't think that it is therefore insignificant. Ten commandments were given at Sinai and our Lord summarized those in terms of two. The multitude of words cannot always be equated with importance. Discipline without the benefit of prayer is unavoidably a prelude to disappointment. There is probably no place where we fail so miserably as Christian parents as upon our knees. May God be pleased to so work in our homes as to strengthen His people and thereby testify to His greatness in the midst of a world of unsaved men. Correction can only be biblical when it is bathed in prayer.

REVIEW

1. What is a steward, and in what sense are parents stewards?
2. What do we hope to accomplish by biblical discipline?
3. What can we do when we run into difficulties as parents?
4. How should we pray for ourselves? For our children?
5. What is the relationship between the rod and prayer?

RESPONSE

1. What am I doing *now* when I become frustrated with my children?
2. What things should I ask the Lord to do within me?
3. Am I praying earnestly for my children? What things should I ask the Lord to do in them?
4. Do I ever pray with my children when I correct them? How soon can I begin?

6

Love and the Rod

In this chapter we want to continue to look at some of the practical aspects of applying biblical discipline in our homes. We have seen that the authority we possess as parents is only *delegated* to us by the Lord, and that our function is to be managers who will bring our children into direct and daily contact with the authority of God Himself. We have also seen that we cannot possibly expect to succeed in our work without unceasing prayer and continual communication with our sovereign Lord. A third principle is that biblical correction must be administered in a context of love.

Love necessitates correction. "Withhold not correction from the child: for if thou beatest him with the rod, he shall not die. Thou shalt beat him with the rod, and shalt deliver his soul from hell" (Prov. 23:13,14 AV). Do we love the children that God has placed under our charge? Do we want to see our children cast into hell, or do we want to see them spared from the wrath of God? If we love them and would see them spared, God says we must administer discipline. Correction is an evidence of love.

In Proverbs 29:15 Solomon writes, "The rod and reproof give wisdom, but a child who gets his own way brings shame to his mother." Do we want our children to be wise? Do we want them to be filled with the wisdom of God? We cannot help them without applying biblical discipline. We cannot help them apart from the rod accompanied by verbal reproof. "The rod and reproof give wisdom."

Again Solomon writes to us in Proverbs 19:18, "Discipline your son while there is hope, and do not desire his death." Do you see how *necessary* it is to administer discipline? It is *literally* a question of life and death! Do you love your children? Then discipline them while there is hope. If you love them, chasten them while they are young, for the hope diminishes as they grow older. Indeed, as long as they are alive there is hope, but the hope fades as we fail in our responsibility to administer discipline from the very earliest months.

Do we *really love* our children? Proverbs 13:24 (AV) says, "He that spareth his rod hateth his son: but he that loveth him chasteneth him betimes" or early. It is the responsibility of fathers, in particular, to see that discipline is administered in the home, and God says that if you love your children you must discipline them. There is no antithesis between love and discipline. Some people tell me that they love their children *too much* to apply the rod. They say that love and discipline are at opposite ends. But it simply is not so. On the authority of God's Word I can say that love expresses itself in discipline because God says, "He who spares his rod hates his son." Despite all protests to the contrary, if we allow our children to go their own way without administering correction, it is a sign to the world, to our child, and to God, that we despise our child's soul and are content to see him continue in his downward spiral toward hell.

Love demands discipline, and biblical discipline can only be administered in a context of love. In fact, biblical correction, like a hug or a kiss, is an emblem to the child of love, security, and acceptance. Did you ever realize that? The loving administration of the rod is an emblem to the child of security. It is an assurance of love. It is an emblem of his acceptance with his parents. Hebrews 12 sets the pattern for us. Remember that we are to administer our authority under God's authority; we are to reflect His manner and attitude. Hebrews 12 describes the manner and attitude of biblical correction as God disciplines His spiritual seed. In Hebrews 12: 6-8 we read, "For those whom the Lord loves He disciplines, and He scourges every son whom he receives. It is for discipline that you endure; God deals with you as with sons; for what son is there whom his father does not discipline? But if you are without discipline, of which all have become partakers, then you are illegitimate children and not sons." Paul encourages us in this passage as Christians that when God afflicts us we should not grow weary of it or despise it, but we should look upon God's chastening hand as an expression of His love. God loves us so much, Christian, that he will not sit idly by as we go off the course. God loves us so much that He will administer the rod of discipline to get us back onto the course where we ought to walk. God chastens every one of His children—in varying degrees to be sure—but He chastens every one of His children, and so the child who is being disciplined by God ought to look upon it as an emblem of his acceptance with Him. It is an assurance, a mark of grace, that God really does care about us and so corrects us when we err. But if we do not see that correction, then it means that God has no fatherly affection toward us. And that's because we're illegitimate. "God gave them up," the Bible says in Romans 1 (AV). This He does to all those who think that they are God's children but who have not been born into His holy family.

The discipline that we administer in our homes is to reflect God's discipline. For our children to be without this sanctifying influence of the rod is for them to be as unclaimed and unloved illegitimate children. Parents who seek to show their affection by setting no restrictions upon their children are in reality treating them as bastards, and not as sons. They are in truth treating them as illegitimate and unwanted. We must say to our children what Christ says to His Church in Revelation 3:19 "Those whom I love, I reprove and discipline; be zealous therefore, and repent." We must say to our children, "Johnny, Mary, those whom I love I reprove and correct. Be zealous therefore. Repent of your way before God. Get on the right course and obey, because God has said that you must."

Notice too that God's discipline is corrective and not merely punitive in nature. Look at verses 12 and 13 of Hebrews 12. "Therefore, strengthen the hands that are weak and the knees that are feeble, and make straight paths for your feet, so that the limb which is lame may not be put out of joint, but rather be healed." God administers discipline not to inflict punishment upon His children, but in order to keep limbs that are lame from being put out of joint and to see them healed. Now to be sure, God's righteousness demands that He punish sin. This He will do on that great dark day of judgment when His anger will grow hot, His mercy will be covered, and He will cast both body and soul into hell. *That is punishment.* But with respect to His children, God's purpose is *always corrective.* It is not retribution or vengeance. He is not afflicting them in order to punish them for the sins which they have committed. He is afflicting them with a view toward correction, toward bringing their feet back to center, toward bringing them to walk that straight and narrow path again.

The fornicator of 1 Corinthians 5 is cast out of the church and is delivered unto Satan for the destruction of the flesh. Why? To punish him for his sins as a taste of hell? It says in 1 Corinthians 5:5 that this was done to the end that "his spirit may be saved in the day of the Lord Jesus." The man was afflicted not for punishment, but for correction, in order that his spirit may be saved. The rod was administered to him physically in order to bring about repentance, but it is not so with the wicked. God punishes the wicked and there is no room for repentance. But God *chastens* His children. While punishment and discipline may at times take the same form, yet the purpose is vitally different. There is grief, pain, and sorrow both in punishment and in discipline. The difference is that in punishment there is no hope, but in chastening the whole purpose is correction. That is important for us to realize.

Paul says concerning Hymenaeus and Alexander that they, too, were delivered unto Satan. Why? To be punished? It says in 1 Timothy 1:20 that this was done so that they might learn not to blaspheme. It was not done that God's retributive justice might be poured out upon them. It was done in order to correct them, in order that they might be taught not to continue in that sin which had carried them away.

Frequently, all too frequently, we lash out at our children because they have embarrassed us or hurt us, and our concern is not so much to correct them as it is to make them suffer for what they have done to us. We are punishing and not correcting whenever we discipline out of embarrassment or anger instead of love. Our concern as parents must be to see our children corrected: to see a change in their attitudes and a change in their actions, to see their lame feet put back onto that course and walking once more in the direction that the Lord would have them pursue. May God forgive us when we seek to turn the authority to correct into a license to abuse; we don't have that right. Any discipline that we administer, any correction that would be biblical, must be administered under God's authority, and it must be administered in a context of love.

As parents we are responsible to control the atmosphere of a spanking and to generate the warmth and the love which is essential to biblical discipline. It is most natural for parent and child to physically and verbally express their love as soon as possible after a spanking—as soon as the child stops crying. The same hand that administers the rod then draws the child to an embrace, assuring the child that the rod was not administered out of hate but out of a heart that loves that child and is concerned for that child's good. Jimmy is confident that, "Daddy spanks me because he loves me." I shudder every time I see a parent administer the rod or spank a child and then leave him like a dog to lick his sores. I shiver every time I see a child turn to his dad for assurance of affection after a spanking, and see that father breathe out coldness, rejection, and anger. It's no wonder, is it, that after a spanking like that some of our children run to their rooms, slam their doors, and cry, "I hate you! I hate you! I hate you!" They need to be assured that we spank them because we love them. They *are* assured of that when, after the spanking, we embrace them, hug them, kiss them, and tell them that we love them and that is why we correct them.

How does the coldness, the anger, the tension, and the hostility which is sensed between father and son reflect God's attitude in chastening His spiritual children? It does not. We have never been disciplined that way by God. God has never afflicted us and then abandoned us. Has He? I challenge anyone who knows Jesus Christ to say, "Jesus Christ chastened me and left me." We cannot say it. On the other hand, if I were to ask some children, "How many of you can say that your parents have disciplined you and abandoned you, made you to feel that your world is falling apart and there's nobody else there to pick up the pieces?," how many of our children would say, "That's true; that's exactly what happens."?

Our responsibility before God is to administer correction under His authority, *accurately* reflecting the manner in which He chastises His beloved sons in love. Biblical correction can only be administered in a context of love; anything else is not biblical correction. It may be discipline, or it may be correction, or it may have a correcting influence, but it is not *biblical* correction. It is not obedient to the command of God.

Another principle of biblical discipline is that physical correction must be administered with sufficient firmness. While it is to be administered under God's authority and in a context of love, yet it is to be done with sufficient firmness to impress the lesson. Again, we must look to God's method of disciplining His people in order to see how we ought to correct our children.

In Acts 5 we have the case of Ananias and Sapphira, a man and his wife who lied to the Holy Spirit and who were subsequently struck down by God as an example to the church. Did the believers take it as a light reproof? Did they go their way laughing after having been spanked by the Lord? Acts 5:11 says, "great fear came upon the whole church, and upon all who heard of these things." Great fear came upon the church: discipline had its desired effect. No man afterwards would lie to the Holy Spirit. Correction was administered firmly for the good of the church. When we take our oldest son aside and spank him, does he go away laughing? Do the other children laugh with him? Does the whole family think it's a big joke? Sometimes we do not see the desired effect of correction because we have not administered discipline with sufficient firmness.

In 1 Corinthians 11, some of the members of the church at Corinth were despising or treating shamefully the body of Christ or other church members. This abuse took place in the context of the Lord's Supper. Some people were getting drunk and filling their stomachs full while others at the opposite end of the table were eating and drinking nothing at the Agape feast which preceded the actual celebration of the ordinance. Therefore, God brought discipline upon the church at Corinth. What form did this discipline take? 1 Corinthians 11:30-32 says, "For this reason [because of your disobedience] many among you are weak and sick, and a number sleep. But if we judged ourselves rightly, we should not be judged. But when we are judged, we are disciplined by the Lord in order that we may not be condemned along with the world." This was not to punish them, but to correct them. Now that's a hard way to be disciplined. It was a stiff lesson to learn, but the principle was reinforced and the church straightened out. God sometimes had to kill people in order to discipline or correct His children!

How much lesser affliction is the discipline which God commands *us* to afflict with the rod. You and I cannot discipline by death; we do not have that authority. Nor do we have the authority to administer sickness in correcting our children. God has given us *the rod,* and *that* is the means by which we are to discipline. It is much less severe than death and disease, but if God on occasion found it necessary to implement *both* death and disease in order to chasten His children, then we ought not to shrink from the rod. "Although you beat him with the rod, he will not die." He may *sound* like it, but he won't. "You shall beat him with the rod, and deliver his soul from Sheol." Again in Proverbs 19:18 (AV), "Chasten thy son while there is hope, and let not thy soul spare for his crying." A man is not a man if he can administer discipline without being broken within. It hurts to be the source of pain for your own children, your own flesh and blood. But God says, "Let not thy soul spare for his

crying." If you beat him with the rod he will cry, but he will
not die. Discipline must be administered with sufficient
firmness.

Certainly it is not possible to establish a standard of firmness and say that a spanking must be so many *kiloswats* hard.
There is no such unit of measurement and there cannot be,
for all the forces involved are variable. Each one of our children has a different level of pain tolerance. Father has a
harder hand than mother. We simply cannot measure by any
definable unit how firm a spanking ought to be. I have seen
some parents (and I know you have, too) discipline their
children by giving them just a little swat on the bottom that
wouldn't even kill a fly if it got in the way! Some parents
discipline their children with what we call *love pats* in our
family. This "discipline" is doomed to fail. It produces no
grief, sorrow, or repentance in the children. They just go
right on doing what they *were* doing, and the parents wonder
why. "Ah, that's it, Judy's tired; that's why she's acting this
way. She's not responding to discipline tonight because she's
tired or not feeling well, or she's had a difficult day." We
make up excuses for our children when what we *need* to do
is to administer firm discipline to which they will respond.

Any correction that would seek to be termed biblical
discipline certainly must meet the *standards* of biblical discipline. In Hebrews 12:11, we discover the minimum requirements for discipline, "All discipline for the moment seems
not to be joyful, but sorrowful; yet to those who have been
trained by it, afterwards it yields the peaceful fruit of righteousness." There are two requirements for biblical discipline
which are established by this verse. Do you see them both?

The first is this: "All discipline for the moment seems not
to be joyful, but sorrowful." There can be no discipline without causing sorrow. Do our children laugh and giggle or play
when they are being disciplined? Then we are not spanking

them hard enough. Do they get angry and cry out against us—
"I don't want a spanking. I don't like you. You're a mean,
nasty person"? Then we've not disciplined them firmly
enough. The marks of biblical discipline are grief and sorrow,
not laughter or anger. "Fathers, do not provoke your children
to anger," but we do provoke them to anger whenever we fail
to discipline with sufficient firmness. When you spank a child
too hard you'll not see anger; he doesn't have the will to be
angry. He's too broken. We need to learn that sufficient degree of firmness where we are neither too hard nor too soft.
We need to *correct;* we need to learn to recognize, with each
one of our children, that point where we have brought grief
and sorrow for their rebellion, for grief and sorrow are the
marks of biblical discipline.

The second mark is also here in verse 11: "All discipline
for the moment seems not to be joyful, but sorrowful; yet to
those who have been trained by it, afterwards it yields the
peaceful fruit of righteousness." "Yet. . .*afterwards* it yields."
If we have properly administered discipline afterwards it
yields—not sometimes, or occasionally, but *unfailingly*—the
peaceful fruit of righteousness to those who have been
trained by it. If we bring grief and sorrow alone to our children, we have failed to administer biblical discipline. Are we
setting a high standard? We are, but the Bible sets the
standard for discipline, and anything that falls short of
that standard is less than biblical discipline. Remember, the
supreme motive for biblical discipline is to bring our child
into a subordinate relationship to the authority of God. Our
whole purpose in using the rod is to bring about obedience
to the commands and precepts of God's Word. Having administered the rod, does our son now obey, or is he still rebellious? Does he immediately do and will he follow through
on that for which he was disciplined, or is he still reluctant
to obey? We have not been firm enough if there is still that

rebellion in his heart. In spite of the grief, sorrow, and tears that may have poured forth, if they do not produce obedience, then we have not yet administered biblical discipline. Does he obey instantaneously and sweetly, or does he obey grudgingly, with that little bit of rebellion still in his heart? A friend remembers his mother saying to his father when he was a child, "Give him some more, Dad, he's not sweet yet." He says that when he was little he didn't quite understand that, but now it all makes sense. Biblical discipline has not been administered until the child obeys unhesitatingly and with the proper attitude. If you have to spank him twice, you did not communicate the message the first time. Do it right the first time and you won't have to spank him again. Do it with sufficient firmness and the peaceful fruit will follow.

Perhaps in some of these passages you've noticed the biblical emphasis on the rod. The rod is an instrument, a tool, a means to help us to administer firm discipline. It may be *literally* a rod (a stick or a switch), or it may be a ping-pong paddle, the belt around your pants, or a ruler (which some parents have found to be quite effective). The hand, while it is probably the instrument most readily available to us, is really one of the most inefficient. When we spank a child with our hand there are several things that may happen. One thing is that all the force which is brought by the downward motion of the arm is spread out over five fat fingers and therefore it doesn't really get through. When you spank your child and he has on a pair of pants and underwear (or perhaps two or three diapers), it takes a little bit of force for that to be felt. It will *not* be felt if it must be spread out over five fingers—at least not effectively.

Another thing that can happen with the hand is that we may jar the child. So much force is required to make the hand felt that we will not only administer affliction to a prescribed area on his bottom; we will also jar his whole body.

Serious injury may result from a careless spanking. I once saw a mother have her daughter bend over a table while she spanked her. The daughter cried, but she held her stomach, not her bottom. The danger of injury is very real. Confine your spankings to that pillowy flesh on the backside. Avoid striking the back (where the spine may be injured), the legs, face, or other parts of the body.

The value of a rod is this: Whether the rod is a ping-pong paddle, switch, stick, belt, or ruler, *all* of the force which is used is confined to that narrow area. It is not spread out over five fat fingers—it is spread out over a ruler that may be an inch wide. It takes *less force* to administer the discipline, and it is more keenly felt. The rod is more accurate, and there is much less likelihood of inflicting the kind of damage that may be caused by excessive force.

The rod can be more effective than the hand, but if you don't happen to carry a ping-pong paddle in your back pocket, that does not mean that you must wait two or three hours until you get home to correct your children. Your hand is there, and if it's the only rod that you have, use it. Use it with care; use it with caution; use it recognizing its built-in limitations and even dangers, but use it because the rod must be administered firmly.

But what about correcting older children? The rod may be just fine for the little ones, but how do you discipline sixth graders and teenagers? All of the principles that we've discussed—God's authority, prayer, love, and even the rod—apply to all children of all ages. Teens are not exceptions to the rule.

The rod is primarily for training. Hebrews tells us that those who are trained by it will enjoy "a harvest of righteousness and peace" (12:11 NIV). Children who are trained by their parents to obey will live at peace with their parents (and other members of the family!) *because* they obey. The parents who enjoy a good relationship with their children during the transitional teenage years are the parents who laid a solid foundation earlier.

The years of real *hope* (Prov. 19:18) are actually much fewer than many of us realize. By the first day of school many of our child's character traits are already set and hardening. "As the twig is bent, so goes the tree." The *storyteller* of kindergarten days will be a hardened *liar* by junior high. That's why it is especially important to begin disciplining children scripturally right away, as soon as they are born. Later on it will be much more difficult, and it may even be *too late*.

When the rod is used diligently in the formative years, it will be used less frequently in the transitional or teenage years. Notice that I said *less frequently*. Don't pack it away yet! As a child matures in a context of loving discipline, he develops an attitude of responsiveness and obedience toward his parents. He soon learns that this is the way to experience peace and joy in the home. Every day he is directly confronted with the claims of God upon him, and as he grows in his knowledge and understanding of the Lord and His Word, he realizes that obedience is the key to peace and joy in all of life. "Trust and obey, for there's no other way." Children love to sing that, and it's true. There's no other way to happiness and peace but to trust and obey.

Don't buy the bill of goods that says that teenage rebellion is *natural* and that these years are *always* painful. Many teenagers actually want to obey their parents *more when they are teenagers* than they did when they were younger. These are years of tremendous physical and emotional changes: of menstruation, peach fuzz, and romance. The teen wants and needs a stable home life. He will rock the boat and try his wings, and to some extent that's good. A sensitive parent will give him some room along with much loving counsel and guidance. But the teen also wants to know the boundaries. How far can he fly? How late can he stay out? Sometimes he feels like a prince; other days he feels like a toad. Do you love him with his pimples and whiskers as much as you loved him *before?* He needs reassurance, the reassurance that you care enough about him to discipline him when he errs. "Those whom I love, I reprove and discipline."

The rod is less prominent now, because he has already been trained to respond in obedience. Verbal reproof will frequently be sufficient to put him back on course. But when it fails, that means he needs to be *retrained.* The rod must be brought back out to physically reinforce the lesson. He doesn't *like* the rod, but he still respects it, and he will respond to it. The rod is a symbol of your loving care and concern: he has been trained with it all his days.

The families that get into trouble are the families that fail to *maintain* loving and consistent discipline throughout the teenage years. Some parents back off when junior grows into a giant and takes up weightlifting. They forget that the authority they have and must exercise is delegated to them by God: it is not theirs because they are bigger, older, or smarter. Junior is confused when his parents lighten up: don't they love him any more? This seed of doubt can grow into a root of bitterness that decades won't be able to heal.

But the rod? Why not go to alternate means of correction, such as denying privileges or grounding? Aren't these more effective with older children than the rod? Recently a very close friend and dear brother came to me with that exact argument. His son had committed a rather serious offence for which he had been *grounded.* For two weeks he was supposed to be isolated from friends and neighbors and to remain in the house. His father said to me, "Somehow it seemed to require more than just a little spanking. Maybe two weeks of thinking about what he did will do him some good."

I agreed with my friend, but only in part. The nature of the offence *did* demand more than just a *little* spanking: biblical correction must be proportionate (see chapter 8). A serious departure requires serious correction. However, I could not agree with him that *grounding* would achieve the desired objectives. *Grounding* fails to qualify as an adequate corrective measure for several reasons.

In the first place, grounding is impossible to enforce. If correction is really going to correct, then it must be enforceable. You can't expect corrective shoes to straighten the foot if you can't make Jimmy wear them. At the very moment that we were talking on my front porch, my friend's son was in the back yard playing ball with my son. The fact that he was able to escape isolation once gave him hope that he could find a loophole again. Thus the certainty of discipline was destroyed (see chapter 10), and his son will never again look upon *grounding* as a serious and inescapable corrective measure. Never make threats that you know you cannot fulfill, or you will soon lose the respect of your children.

Secondly, the practice of grounding allows a sinful and unnatural tension to remain between the child and his parents for days or even weeks. Mom and Dad have to maintain a cool and negative attitude toward their son or daughter to even *think* of trying to enforce grounding. That coldness destroys everything that was established in the earlier part of this chapter. That negative attitude seeks to hurt, not to correct, and it thus fails to accurately reflect the chastening hand of God.

Thirdly, the Scriptures provide for that situation where physical correction of itself is deemed to be inadequate.

The scriptural principle is not grounding: it is *restitution*. Restitution is seen, for example, in Exodus 22:1, where the thief who steals an ox and sells it must restore fivefold to the owner. "But my son didn't *steal* anything; he just threw some rocks at a girl in the neighborhood." That may be true, but then *restitution* is not only for the thief. It is for any situation where person or property has been harmed or endangered. Thus, if somebody starts a fire, and it consumes a neighboring grainfield, "he who started the fire shall surely make restitution." If your son threw rocks at the girl down the street, or put a BB through Mrs. Jackson's window, or rode his bike through her flowerbed, then he ought to be made to do something especially nice for the person whose property he harmed or endangered (including, of course, the replacement of any property that was destroyed). The function of correction is to rescue the child from his wrongful course and to establish him on the proper path wherein he assumes personal responsibility for his actions. *Grounding* will not do that; *restitution* as a part of biblical correction will. Restitution demands an immediate, personal, and proper response, whereas *grounding* provides only time for thought (perhaps to plot revenge).

"But," said my friend, "maybe two weeks of thinking about what he did will do him some good." It is far more likely that he will be thinking about how unfair and mean his parents are, or how to escape the yoke of bondage that they've placed upon him, or how to do the same thing again without getting caught, than about how to avoid the offence that brought his troubles upon him. Physical correction and restitution are quick and effective corrective measures. *Grounding* is slow, torturous, and falls short of biblical correction. It's interesting that recent surveys confirm that many teens would rather be disciplined by the rod and forgiven than to endure the alienation of methods such as *grounding*.

Let us pray together that God may so work in us that we lovingly, yet firmly, correct our children and thereby become the means of delivering their souls from hell. May God be pleased to work in you fathers, mothers, and teachers, to learn how to do your job and to do it well; and may God be pleased to work in the hearts of your children to bring them to a knowledge of Jesus Christ, to save them from their sins, to enable them to obey you and to do that which is right in His sight.

REVIEW

1. Can we love our children *too much* to discipline them?
2. How is biblical correction an emblem of love and assurance?
3. Where do we find the true model for biblical discipline?
4. What is the difference between punishment and correction?
5. How can we know when a spanking is firm enough? What are the two marks of successful correction?
6. Why is the hand not efficient and sometimes dangerous in discipline?
7. Why does *grounding* fail to qualify as biblical correction?
8. How can we discipline teenagers?

RESPONSE

1. Do I demonstrate love and affection toward my children when I discipline them?
2. Am I frequently satisfied with a response that is less than repentance and obedience?
3. Do I *punish* or *correct* my children?
4. Am I firm enough?
5. Do I use a rod? Should I? Are there *other* practices I need to correct?

7

The Rod and Reproof

A fifth characteristic of biblical discipline is that *physical correction must be accompanied by verbal reproof.* Too many parents spank their children without ever actually telling them why. Years later I meet their grown children in my office for counseling that *could* have been avoided. One man told me that whenever his mother became angry with him she spanked him and then gave him the *cold shoulder* treatment for days and even weeks at a time. If he asked her what he had done to upset her so, she would reply matter of factly, "You know." But he really *didn't* know. He didn't understand because she never told him.

In cases such as this one the rod may have been applied, but there was no biblical discipline. Biblical discipline is *correction,* and that means that the pattern of the child's behavior must be *changed by instruction* in righteousness. He must be shown the error of his way, and then directed to the proper path. This requires explanation and instruction. Biblical discipline demands words.

Discipline can in some ways be likened to preaching a sermon. It is a message revealing the nature of God, the sin of man, and the consequences that necessarily follow. But try to imagine a sermon without words. The preacher is fervent, emphatic, and quite energetic. But it's all meaning-less. The message of the gospel cannot be communicated by pounding the pulpit or waving your arms in the air: *we need words*. So do our children. If we do not take the time to tell them what they did wrong and what they *ought* to do, then our discipline is nothing more than a painful pantomime. Spanking without words, like preaching without words, is utterly useless as a means of grace. It *cannot* have its desired effect.

"The rod and reproof give wisdom" (Prov. 29:15). Neither one can do the job by itself. The rod without words fails to teach our children the difference between right and wrong. Words without the rod become shallow, empty air. We must be certain that our children always understand the exact rea-son they are being disciplined.

It may not be possible each and every time, but whenever circumstances permit we ought to have a full discussion with our child incorporating the following elements:

First, be certain that he understands what he did that was wrong. Let *him* figure it out: make him think. If he needs a little help, then give it to him. "Jimmy, what did you do?" "I hit Susan," or "I called Freddy a bad name." Have him *be specific*. Don't settle for "I disobeyed," or "I did something I wasn't supposed to do." Those very general answers don't tell us that he really understands. They may simply be his reaction to the circumstances. He knows that he is disciplined when he disobeys. He is being disciplined; therefore he must have disobeyed. If he does not know *specifically* what he is being corrected for, he will not be corrected. If he doesn't understand, you can count on him to do it again.

Second, bring the authority of God to bear on him di-rectly. Ask him a question. "What does *God* say about that?" Again, give *him* the opportunity to respond. Let him search his mind to see if he can recall the teaching of Scripture. If he cannot, then we need to help him. This is our opportunity to do what we talked about earlier, to apply specific texts directly to his behavior. "Jimmy, why did you punch Susan? Don't you remember that God says, 'A gentle answer turns away wrath'?" Or, in the other situation we described, "Jimmy, James says that the tongue 'is a restless evil and full of deadly poison.' I know you've heard that 'Sticks and stones may break my bones, but names can never hurt me.' But that's not true. Broken bones can be set and put into a cast to mend, but 'death and life are in the power of the tongue.' How do you suppose Freddy feels right now?" When he's broken a commandment of the Lord, remind him of that commandment and what it means. Help him to see that by what he has done he has offended God. After you have done this a few times, you will be genuinely surprised at his response. We are establishing a pattern and giving scriptural direction to his conscience. Soon he will be able to recognize his sins himself, and he will see them as sins against the Lord. This is exactly what we want to accomplish in discipline.

Third, help him to evaluate his own actions in the light of Scripture. Ask him another question. "Well, then, has your action been right or wrong (good or bad) according to the Scriptures?" We need to teach our children how to discern right from wrong. Many people never learn how to do that. They seem to think that discernment is a gift that some people have and that others lack. God has given us a touchstone in the Scriptures. In the old days a miner could test the purity of gold or silver by rubbing it against a type of black stone and then examining the streak that was left on it. We can judge the actions and ideas of all men by rubbing them against the Scriptures to test their purity. Our children need to be trained in this from their earliest days. By this procedure they will learn that *you* are not judging them;

God is, through His Word. And remember, "If we judged ourselves rightly, we should not be judged [of the Lord]" (1 Cor. 11:31).

Fourth, help him to see that when he sins he needs to be corrected. Another question: "What happens when you disobey?" His answer again ought to be something specific: "I need to be spanked," or "I need to be disciplined." It is important for our children to recognize—and verbalize—that discipline is something that they really do *need,* as much as they need three meals a day and a good night's sleep. Correction is essential to their development and something that they will experience all of their lives. The Lord disciplines us "for our good" (Heb. 12:10), and our children need to see discipline as a good part of their lives.

Fifth, show to him your obligation to be God's agent in correction. I always make it a point to ask my children, "As your father, what *must I do* under God's authority?" My children reply, "You ought to spank me." Now it's clear. Our child has violated God's commandments, and he therefore needs to be corrected under God's authority delegated to us as parents. He realizes that we don't have any choice. We are under authority, just as he is. We are required to correct him when he errs, and if we don't, then we will ourselves be disciplined by the Lord. Our children need to know that we discipline them as agents of God, and not because we enjoy using the rod.

Finally, after we have spanked him and loved him, we can *explain to him what he ought to do* so that he may avoid having to be corrected in the future.

Here are those questions again.

What did you do?

What does *God* say about this?

Was what you did right or wrong according to the Scriptures?

What happens when you disobey?

What *must I do* as a parent under God's authority?

What ought you to do in the future?

We will, of course, have to adjust the details of such a discussion to suit the different ages and circumstances of our children, but the thrust of what we say must be the same whether we are dealing with a child of fourteen months or fourteen years. Little children and big children, even grown children, must hear words that tell them why they are being disciplined by their parents, or by the Lord.

REVIEW

1. What is the purpose of *correction?*
2. How is the rod without reproof like preaching without words?
3. What elements do we need to incorporate in reproof?
   a.
   b.
   c.

d.

e.

f.

RESPONSE

1. Am I certain that my children understand why I correct them?
2. Do I take the time to really talk with them about discipline?
3. Which of the elements listed above do I need to concentrate on with my children?

8

Discipline by Measure

A sixth principle is that biblical correction must be proportionate in its application. Let me explain what I mean by that. The fact that physical discipline must be *sufficiently firm* to impress the lesson *does not mean* that it must be *equally firm* for every lesson.

One wheel slightly over the yellow line as I'm driving along the highway does not require nearly the effort to correct that would be demanded if my entire car had been allowed to drift into the opposing lane and I were facing oncoming cars and certain destruction. A sharp angle of departure requires a sharp action to restore me to my proper path. A sudden pull to the left requires a firm pull to the right to bring me back into my own lane on the highway. I must be careful not to either over-correct or under-correct. If I over-correct by pulling on the wheel too sharply, I risk running off the road. And if I under-correct by not turning sharply enough, I'll still be mangled by that truck whose headlights are bearing down on me. An error in either direction may be fatal: my correction must be proportionate to my mistake.

This is true in the spiritual realm as well. During Bible times God had to physically afflict and even kill people in order to correct the situation. I'm glad that He more frequently reproves and chastens us in gentle firmness by the application of His Word. Sometimes the departure is so sharp that God must bring death to a church in order to correct His children. But normally the preaching of the Word is sufficient to restore them to the proper path.

That is the way it ought to be with our correction in the home. There are some offenses which can be corrected by a sharp glance from one of the parents. The children know what that means and they know that they had better straighten out.

There are some offenses for which all you need to do is to *snap your fingers,* if you train your children to respond to that signal. When Nathan had just begun to crawl, we wanted to teach him to stay in one room. We didn't want him going where we couldn't see him. So we trained him to respond to a snap of the fingers. Whenever he began to go out the door we just snapped our fingers and he stopped. He knew that signal meant to stop whatever he was doing and look at us for a word of guidance or direction. Then we could signal him to come back, move away from the door, and tell him what he ought to be doing. The *snap* can be used well past the crawling stage in every period of childhood. Our children still respond to it. Whenever they hear fingers snap, they stop and look to us for further instructions. This is a wonderful signal in a department store or other public place. You can discipline without being noticed. A word from the parent will frequently be sufficient to correct the situation.

Most acts of disobedience can be handled by a normal spanking, one with just enough firmness to impress the lesson. But others are of such a serious nature that only a severe spanking can sufficiently impress the lesson upon the mind and the heart of the child. A good friend says that he never used the belt on his son until the day that he lied to him.

Then he felt that the sharpness of the departure was so great that only a severe application of the rod could sufficiently impress the lesson.

The severity of the spanking, then, ought to be in proportion to the seriousness of the departure. If it is only a minor departure, then a glance, a snap, a word, or a normal spanking may be sufficient to bring him back onto the proper path. But if it is a very sharp departure, it may require a very severe pressure to bring him back onto the proper path.

Charles Bridges has well said that the rod "is medicine, not food; the remedy for the occasional diseases of the constitution, not the daily regimen for life and nourishment. To convert medicine into daily food gradually destroys its remedial quality." If every time you put your child across the knee you spank him as hard as you possibly can, he becomes accustomed to that level of spanking and it becomes very, very difficult to impress upon him the seriousness of a future offense. In our home we normally use a ruler, and we reserve a belt for more serious offenses.

Bridges further warns us that "children become hardened under an iron rod. Sternness and severity of manner close up their hearts. It is most dangerous to make them afraid of us." Our children ought to have a healthy respect and fear of the rod. They ought to fear being spanked. They ought to fear bringing displeasure to their parents and to God, but it is a very dangerous thing to make our children *afraid of us*.

The rod needs to be administered in a context of love proportionately according to the seriousness of the departure and also according to the frame of the child. It may be difficult, but we must *learn* to gear the rod to the seriousness of the offense. To continually bear down on our children with a heavy hand without making any distinction between offenses will frustrate them, exasperate them, and cause them to lose heart. Paul had all this in mind when he wrote to parents in Colosse, saying, "Fathers, provoke not your children to anger, lest they be discouraged" (Col. 3:21 AV). When we over-correct, our children lose hope. They begin to feel that we are always *down on them* and that they can do no good in our sight. Use great care and caution: we don't want to run them off the road!

REVIEW

1. Should the correction be the same for every offence?
2. What are some different means of directing our children?
3. What may happen if we come down too hard on our children?

RESPONSE

1. Do I distinguish between offences?
2. What are some things that I regard as more serious than others?
3. Have I been using the rod as medicine or as food?
4. Are my children afraid of me? What must I do to correct this?

9

Correction Within Reason

A seventh principle is that biblical correction must be applied according to reasonable expectations. Again the model for all of our correction as parents must be the chastisement by which God corrects His spiritual seed. Psalm 103:13-14 declares, "Just as a father has compassion on his children, so the Lord has compassion on those who fear Him." Why? "For He Himself knows our frame; He is mindful that we are but dust." We must learn the frame of each one of our children. They are each unique physically, spiritually, and emotionally. There are many highly individual factors which must be considered when we are dealing with our children.

Are they physically capable of meeting our expectations? Are they tall enough? Are they strong enough? Are they coordinated enough to do what we ask? This does not apply only to the little ones who are just learning to walk and to use their muscles. In the transition between childhood and adulthood, many teens go through an awkward period of physical clumsiness. Not every spilled glass at the dinner table is the result of being careless. Sometimes it is a lack of physical coordination. As parents we need to be able to discern the true cause. Was Jimmy being careless, or is he going through this period of physical awkwardness so that he sometimes bumps into tables and drops things? We must be sensitive to the individual development and level of achievement of each one of our children.

We must also ask if they are mentally capable of meeting our expectations. To use an admittedly rather farfetched example, should I expect my three-year-old daughter to be able to carry the basket downstairs and to put an entire load of clothes through the washing machine, and then spank her when she fails to obey? This is an extreme example to be sure, but listen—at this point she has many physical abilities. In fact, with the aid of a chair, she possesses all of the *physical* requirements that are necessary to perform such a task. Joanna has the strength and energy required to carry things. She can climb and put things into the washing machine, and she loves to turn buttons. She could conceivably do it. *She has the physical ability* to do it, but my three year old does *not have the mental ability* to be able to coordinate all the different activities that are physically required and to put them in the right order so as to be able to put through a load of wash in the washing machine. There are many different areas in which this applies. Are our children actually capable, mentally able, to meet our expectations? Do we ask them to do things which they are incapable of understanding or of coordinating mentally? Biblical discipline must be applied according to reasonable expectations.

Yet this principle must not be used as an excuse to avoid discipline. All too frequently we are willing to say that our children cannot understand or do what we expect them to do. Parents who have children under the age of one will be tempted to conclude that their baby is incapable of understanding and therefore ought not to be corrected when he disobeys. That is a deadly mistake. The fact that your baby cannot speak does not mean that he cannot understand. There are many persons who come from foreign countries who cannot speak our language but who can understand quite well what is being said. We can never conclude that because someone cannot speak the language that that necessarily means he cannot understand it. Infants understand much more than we are willing to give them credit for. The infant needs the rod of reproof just as much as the older child, for the Bible tells us that "the wicked are estranged from the womb" (Ps. 58:3). Furthermore, they go astray as soon as they are born, speaking lies. From the time that they are first on mother's breast they should be learning the meaning of the word *no*. When we see that he understands the meaning of the word *no,* then each time that he disobeys we need to be a little bit firmer, until we see that peaceful fruit of obedience.

Neither tiredness nor illness ought to be allowed to remove the sanctifying influence of the rod. Tiredness or illness may be contributing factors. They may tend to make the child sluggish or cranky, but disobedience must still be seen as a basic manifestation of the sin nature, and every manifestation of the sin nature must be corrected. A failure to maintain the rod under these circumstances will produce one of two results.

In the first place, the child will learn to feign tiredness or illness in order to avoid a spanking when he is disobedient. Some will become convincing young actors. If *he* doesn't fake it, *we may* in order to cover up for him. "Oh, she's so tired today. I won't spank her this time. But Sally, don't do that any more." Usually we fall back on this when we're embarrassed by the behavior of our children and want some kind of escape. That's a serious mistake, because the child will learn that he's not spanked when he's tired or not feeling well. Then when he disobeys and we come toward him in order to spank him he will come to us and say, "Mommy, my head hurts," or "Daddy, I'm tired," and think that he can thereby escape the rod. Weariness or illness must never be acceptable excuses for sinful behavior.

In the second place, it may be tremendously difficult to restore discipline when genuine illness or tiredness passes. When he gets out of hand because he's tired or ill it will be tremendously difficult to reapply the rod to get him back into shape when he is feeling better. Rather we ought to maintain the discipline of the rod during all periods of sickness or fatigue. We will want to apply the rod proportionately, recognizing that his illness may be contributing to his disobedience. Perhaps the firmness of our spanking will be somewhat milder, but the rod must still be applied consistently lest he find a way to escape. "Do not hold back discipline from the child, although you beat him with the rod, he will not die" (Prov. 23:13). That is just as true when he is tired or sick as it is when he is energetic and well.

Perhaps a good rule of thumb is to put a child to bed immediately whenever he claims to be tired or sick. This is not intended to be punitive: I am firmly opposed to all *isolationist* techniques. But it may be corrective. If a child is genuinely tired or ill, then what he needs is rest, regardless of his age or the time of day. Children should be taught about the body's need for rest, and sending them to bed should never be used in place of the rod. But if the child is faking, then when you send him to bed after spanking him, he will soon learn that pretending doesn't pay. He was spanked anyway, and on top of that he was sent to bed! That's something he never wants, unless he's genuinely ready for it.

Incidentally, it is not unreasonable to hold children responsible for having *poor attitudes*. Parents who correct wrong behavior often miss the larger issue of attitude. We tend to think that we don't have any control over our inward attitude, but we do. The Apostle Paul said, "the spirits of prophets are subject to prophets" (1 Cor. 14:32), indicating that we can and must control ourselves. Self-control is a mark of maturity, and one of the things which we must teach to our children.

An unbridled attitude provides the energy for sinful behavior. Look again at the events preceding the first murder. Cain was a farmer and his brother Abel was a shepherd. One day they both brought offerings to the Lord. Abel's sacrifice was acceptable to the Lord, while Cain's was not. The Scripture says, "So Cain became very angry and his countenance [lit. his face] fell" (Gen. 4:5). Cain's attitude was written on his face for everyone to see.

The Lord reproved him, seeking to correct both his attitude and his behavior. "Why are you angry? And why has your countenance fallen? If you do well, will not your countenance be lifted up? And if you do not well, sin is crouching at the door; and its desire is for you, but you must master it" (Gen. 4:6,7).

There it is. Cain must control his attitude, or it will surely lead to greater sin. His response *ought* to be to make the proper sacrifice. Then *his* offering will be accepted too.

But Cain would not control his attitude. He brooded. He fed and nurtured his jealousy until one day "when they were in the field . . . Cain rose up against Abel his brother and killed him" (Gen. 4:8).

A wrong attitude must be corrected *before* it leads to greater sin. Don't be afraid to discipline your children for their attitudes, as well as for their actions. They need to learn self-control.

If discipline is to be administered under God's authority, then our children must learn that God is displeased with sin under any and all circumstances. He will not hold men guilt-less because they are tired or not feeling well. If we love our children then we must not permit anything to interfere with the correction that God says is necessary. *Discipline must be reasonable, but discipline must be.*

REVIEW

1. How can we determine reasonable expectations for our children?
2. Can illness or fatigue excuse sin?
3. Is correction limited to outward behavior, or can we deal also with inward attitudes?

RESPONSE

1. In what areas do I expect things from my children that they are physically or mentally unable to do?
2. Do I ever excuse their behavior because they are tired or sick?
3. What should I do when my child says he's tired?
4. Do I ever send my children to bed to punish them or because I don't want them around? Is that right? What should I do?

10

Persevering Consistency

An eighth principle is that biblical correction must be applied with persevering consistency. "Withhold not correction from the child." It is not the *severity* of the correction which will produce obedience; it is the *certainty* of correction which will bring about the desired result. Be consistent in your administration of discipline. Never, never, never issue a warning or a command without following it through.

We should expect instant obedience on the part of our children, and we should reinforce that expectation with the rod each and every time that they fail to obey. Don't fall into the trap of constructing some kind of *early warning system.* There are some parents who have to tell their children to do something two or three times before they will do it. Other parents have to raise their voices beyond the normal range before their children will listen. And still others have to count to three before their children will obey. "If you don't do this by the time I count to three, you're really going to get it." They count, "1–2–the child doesn't move–2½" and so it goes. The child has won. Expect instant obedience and do not implement any kind of early warning system.

There are times when the very lives of our children may depend upon their obeying us immediately. I read of one such instance that occurred in Southern California when a family was camping on their vacation. They were staying in a campsite and the children were out playing on some rocks nearby. As the father scanned the area to see where his two boys were, his eyes fastened upon five-year-old Michael, who had unknowingly cornered a rattlesnake. The rattlesnake was coiled and ready to strike. The father said firmly "Mike, stand still." The boy froze in his tracks when he heard the command of his father. He obeyed instantly. His father then got a rifle and shot the snake. What do you suppose might have happened if it had been necessary for the father to say, "Mike, if you don't stand still by the time I count to three, you're going to be in a lot of trouble." His son's life would have been in danger. There are times when our children's very lives will be in danger unless they learn to obey instantly.

Our children will not respond to our voice the first time in a crisis unless they are accustomed to responding to it the first time under normal circumstances. Our children ought to know that we mean it the very first time that we say it, or they will never believe it until we count to three, say it twice, or raise our voice. Train your children to expect to obey the first time you say something and when you say it in a normal tone of voice. When they do not obey, correct them.

Persevering consistency is no easy job. It will require a great amount of effort to maintain. Set Proverbs 13:24 before your eyes continually, "He who spares his rod hates his son, but he who loves him disciplines him diligently." Resolve that before God your children will know how much you love them by the way in which you consistently and diligently correct them.

Persevering consistency is not easy, and we need to be aware of the things that would draw us away from it.

There will be a tendency to correct diligently every *major* act of disobedience but to take a more casual attitude toward the *minor* acts. But just as God in His holiness cannot overlook sin, we as parents responsible to reflect God's attitude must be careful to correct every act of sinful disobedience however great or small it may seem to be.

Almost 100 years ago, J. C. Ryle warned his hearers, "Beware of letting small faults pass unnoticed under the idea it is a little one. There are no little things in training children; all are important. Little weeds need plucking up as much as any. Leave them alone and they will soon be great." How many of us have gardens in our back yards? Have you weeded those gardens with persevering consistency, or have you allowed some weeds to go the whole summer? Try to pluck them out now. It was easy when the roots were small and didn't go very deep. But to pluck those weeds out now is a backbreaking job because they've been overlooked for so long.

So it is with our children. Allow them to get away with the little things now. You pick up after them, Mom. You pick up all their toys, their socks, and their dirty clothes. When they get married the very things that you overlooked may well be major causes of irritation and conflict in their marriage. A child that is allowed to be a slob when he is young will be a slob when he is older, and much marriage counseling is concerned with this very truth. Most problem marriages are not in trouble because of big things, but because of a lot of little things that add up.

These little things could have been corrected very easily when they were children. That is our responsibility—every little thing. Tell your child to pick up all of his toys. If he leaves a truck or a car sitting out in the middle of his room, point it out to him, and if he still leaves it, discipline him. He is to pick up *every* toy. Be certain that he is aware of

where they are, but then see that he picks them all up.
Discipline him for every little thing. That's why correction is
not easy but very hard. There are going to be days when it
seems like all we do is pick on Jimmy. But those days, difficult though they may be, will pay off in the long run. We
have to be willing to put in those days so that Jimmy may
grow to maturity in the Lord. Persevering consistency is
tremendously important

This tendency to overlook disobedience is frequently
related to the emotional makeup of the parent. Some of us
have what I call a *teapot temper*. A teapot temper is characterized by outward calm but inward turmoil. Outwardly
everything seems fine, but inwardly a lot of little things are
beginning to agitate and boil until finally a lot of noise es-
capes from that little hole in the top of the kettle. Suddenly
we blow up and grab little Jimmy. We throw him across our
knee and then really let him have it, giving him a spanking
like he has never had before in his life. Somehow we think
that that one spanking is going to make up for all the little
irritating things that Jimmy has done throughout the day.
But it just doesn't work that way. We have administered
the rod, yes, but not any kind of correction. Jimmy doesn't
remember half of those little things he did. He can't relate
the spanking to any of those things except, perhaps, the last.
If we've been letting him get away with a lot of things during
the day and suddenly we release all the pressure that has
built up in us upon him, that's *punishment*. The spanking is
a release for *us*, not correction for *him*. We're taking out our
frustrations upon his bottom, that's all.
Nothing can substitute for persevering consistently. A
good spanking at the end of the day can never make up for
the spankings that ought to have been administered throughout the day. We who have teapot tempers must especially be
aware that we need the grace of God to act contrary to the

nature which we possess and in harmony with the Word of God.

Then, too, *discouragement* will tend to draw us away from persevering consistency. It sometimes seems as though we spank and spank with all diligence, but Jimmy doesn't act any better than the children of those permissive parents up the street. Sometimes it seems as though we spend all our time correcting, but Jimmy isn't any better for all of our efforts and all of our time spent in this matter. Charles Bridges well advises us, *"Persevere notwithstanding apparently unsuccessful results."* It is our responsibility to obey God. If God says that we should not hold back discipline from our children, then we must obey and look to Him for the increase. That's *His* job; our job is to do what God says and then leave the results to Him. What to us may be apparently unsuccessful may be a part of the plan of God in bringing our child to Himself. God will give the increase, if we simply obey Him. "Trust in the Lord with all your heart, and do not lean on your own understanding" (Prov. 3:5).

But if our discipline seems to be consistently unsuccessful, perhaps we ought to ask ourselves some questions: "Am I really obeying God? Am I doing my part? Am I administering my discipline conscientiously, applying God's authority directly and constantly to my child? Am I following the administration of the rod with a loving embrace, showing my child that I discipline him because I love him and because I want him to be related to God? Or do I, after the rod, resent my child and cut him off and act coldly toward him? Am I being firm enough in the administration of the rod?"

One father told me that his correction was apparently unsuccessful. He was getting no place with his child until finally one day he pulled his son's pants down and then used the rod. Then it began to work because finally his child felt it. Between a pair of pants, rubber pants, and two sets of diapers, he wasn't feeling the rod. The father thought he was using it with all firmness, but it wasn't getting through. Examine the way in which you spank. Is it getting the message across? Is your child feeling it? Is it causing grief and sorrow, followed by sweet submission—the marks of biblical correction? Today that father who learned to take his son's pants down is rejoicing. He doesn't have to spank his son nearly as often, and the spankings are much more effective. His son is already much more obedient. Biblical correction works.

Sometimes when things aren't going quite right we can run through the check list and still not locate the problem. Frequently the answer will be to persevere in what we are doing. Just hang in there.

One day we took Susanna to the bank, and the teller gave her a lollipop. She wouldn't say, "Thank you," so we made her return the lollipop. Then we took her outside where we talked to her, spanked her, and loved her. When we took her back into the bank, we promptly went through the whole thing again. Susanna still refused to say, "Thank you."

As the day progressed it became apparent that this would be a very crucial test in her life. Susanna was the most stubborn of our children. She was determined that no matter how many times we spanked her, she would *not* say, "Thank you." For three long days we put her into situations where she knew she had to say those words, and when she didn't, we spanked her. Those were three of the most miserable days of my life. I didn't know what else to do, except to persevere in consistency. Finally, on the third day, she said it. What a time of rejoicing for all of us! And what a change in Susanna! She was so happy that she phoned one of the women in the church and said, "Aunt Nancy, I obeyed. I said 'thank you', and now I'm happy!"

Discipline is a way for us to live happily with our children in this fallen world. When we correct sin, then we are free to enjoy our children and they are free to enjoy us. Families who don't know the joys of biblical discipline are in bondage. Keep it up. When you don't know what to do, keep on doing what you *do* know, and trust the Lord for the results.

REVIEW

1. Is it the severity or the certainty of correction that produces obedience?
2. Is instant obedience unrealistic? Should we give our children hints to tell them when we are serious?
3. What are some things that draw us away from perseverence?
   a.
   b.
   c.
4. When we don't know what to do, what should we do?

RESPONSE

1. Am I consistent or sporadic in my approach to discipline?
2. Do I have an *early warning system?* What is it? How can I get rid of it?
3. What factors hinder me from being consistent? What can I do to overcome them?

11

Partners in Management

In Genesis 1, when God created male and female in His image, He gave to *both of them* (vss. 26, 28) the command to subdue the earth and to rule or manage it under his authority. In the fuller account of the creation of man and woman given in Genesis 2, the woman is made to be a helper for the man in the work of management. The woman shares with the man in the work and responsibility of management. There is no place where this can be seen more clearly than in the home. If there is to be any kind of godly discipline in the home, both parents must work together. Mom and Dad have to agree how to discipline their children. And this agreement must be much more than theoretical. Both parents must practice it consistently.

Instant obedience will only be gained as the fruit of instant correction. Discipline must never be delayed, for postponement may give our children hope that it will never come to pass. Men today interpret Christ's delay as meaning that He will never come and that they will never suffer judgment or punishment for their sins. Of course that is a perverted hope, and we must be careful not to give our children reason to hope in a similar fashion.

In Dad's absence, Mom should apply the rod just as firmly as if it were his hand. Wives should avoid the pattern of threatening, "You just wait 'til your father gets home, and then see what happens!" What *will* happen? Danny will look at the clock on the wall and figure out how many hours there are before Dad gets home. Then he'll do one of two things. Either he'll be good as gold for the remainder of the day, hoping that Mom will forget about her threat, or else he'll figure that he's going to get it anyway, and *really* let loose! In either event, Mom has lost. And so has Danny.

Another problem with this approach is that it makes Mom look like a weak, silly woman, and Dad is a terrible monster who always blows up when he comes home. Again, Mom, Dad, and Danny have all lost. This is not a healthy attitude for a child to have toward his parents. Danny must learn that he is to obey Mother just as quickly as he is to obey Dad, and that she will follow through with the rod just as quickly and as firmly as he will. Parents must work together in the home.

The woman's authority is a *delegated* authority, but it is nonetheless a very *real* authority. If Danny ever senses that Dad won't back up Mom with his arm, it spells disaster for the whole family. We can never allow our sons or daughters to be disrespectful or abusive toward their mother. Talking back must always be treated as a most serious offense. God's Law makes it a capital offense, punishable by death. "And he who strikes his father or his mother shall surely be put to death. And he who curses his father or his mother shall surely be put to death" (Exod. 21:15, 17). There would certainly be many weeping families if this law were carried out today. The time to stop it is when it begins, and Dad has to be the one to do it.

Being partners in management also means that each parent must be aware of what the other one is doing. This is often lacking. Little Danny is no dummy. Our children are not ignorant. Most of them are very bright and smart, and quite skilled at playing one parent against the other. If Danny asks Mom for 15 cents to buy a popsicle and she says *no*, Danny will go out to the garage where Dad is working and ask him the same question. If this ploy works, Danny is set for life. He knows where to go for an easy touch. Our youngest daughter tests us occasionally to see if there's a crack in the solidarity. Always check with your spouse to see if he or she has already answered the question. And if Mom has already said *no*, then Dad needs to discipline Danny for even *attempting* to outmaneuver his parents. After a few sessions with the rod Danny will get the idea that whatever one parent says, the other will stand by it.

At this point a word of caution needs to be mentioned. If we need to check with our spouse, *we* should generally do the checking. Danny sometimes feels like a ping-pong ball. He asks Mom, who sends him to Dad, who sends him back to Mom, and so on until Danny is thoroughly confused. He doesn't know what's up or down, or who's running the home. If no policy has been worked out ahead of time, then it's up to Dad to legislate what will be done.

What should you do if you disagree? Take it up with your spouse privately later, or ask for a few minutes aside if the matter is urgent. But stand firm and united before the children. Children look to their parents as a unit to give them guidance and direction. They must not see cracks where they can drive a wedge between Mom and Dad. Parents must work together and stand together as partners in managing the home.

REVIEW

1. When were husband and wife made partners in management?
2. What is the wife's part in discipline?
3. Is it right to delay discipline? Why or why not?
4. Is it important to maintain a united front?
5. What should you do when you disagree with your spouse?

RESPONSE

1. How actively involved am I in disciplining my children?
2. How can I better support my husband or wife at home?
3. How do I handle disagreements about discipline?
4. Have we established a policy of discipline that we both agree to practice?

12

Children in the Congregation

The church is an extended spiritual family where believers must exhort, encourage, and help one another in disciplining our children. I praise God for the renewed interest across our land in the doctrines of grace, but I fear that much of the impact of Reformed truth will be lost if people look into our homes and see that reformation in doctrine has not made our children any different in behavior than their own.

In an article printed in the *Banner of Truth* magazine, Pastor Albert N. Martin warns us: "Considering that men are so naturally opposed to the doctrines of grace, and living in a day when Arminianism has had the field and there is suspicion, if people can look to the homes of Reformed Christians and see there a structure of order and a cohesion and a respect for authority that stands out in direct contrast to the shoddiness and shallowness of the man-centered kind of thinking that has permeated our churches, it will be one of the most powerful arguments for the truths we claim to believe, and one of the most effective ways to shut the mouths of our gainsayers. But without it, dear fellow ministers of the gospel and fellow Christians who love the Reformed truth, the truth of the Scriptures, much of what we say will be abortive and come to naught."

The manner in which our children conduct themselves in the worship service, school, neighborhood, and home reflects upon the truth which is proclaimed from the pulpit of our church. It reflects upon the truth which is revealed in the Bible. If unbelievers look at our homes and do not see any greater degree of godliness in our homes than in theirs, they will say that our Book is a failure, our Christ is a failure, and the truths we maintain are not practical. That is a very great responsibility to bear. Under God, I do not want *my home* or *my life* to be the cause of someone outside the church of Jesus Christ saying that God's Word is not true. We have a responsibility before God to so order our homes that they bear witness to the truth. And that responsibility has not only been placed upon us as individuals, but also as churches. We are responsible to help and encourage one another in disciplining our children.

For the cause of truth and for the sake of the Gospel of Jesus Christ, this is an area where we must be free to exhort one another daily. Yet frequently this is the very area where we are least free to speak. J. C. Ryle once commented, "As a minister, I cannot help remarking that there is hardly any subject about which people seem so tenacious as they are about their children. I have sometimes been perfectly astonished at the slowness of sensible Christian parents to allow that their own children are in fault, or deserve blame. There are not a few persons to whom I would far rather speak about their own sins, than tell them their own children had done anything wrong." May God deliver us from that attitude.

It is not healthy when a minister of the Gospel is afraid to help and instruct people how to raise their children. When we are not free to help one another, it is not spiritual good that is being generated. Raising children is an area where we all need help. Surely those who are our brothers and sisters, and our fathers and mothers in Christ Jesus ought to be able to come to our aid without ruffling our feathers.

It is especially when the church gathers for worship that we can all be of help to one another. The age at which parents begin to take their children into worship services will of course vary from church to church. Some churches don't provide any nursery. Others have a nursery for children up to the age of two or three. One church bulletin advertised a nursery for babies 18 months or younger, and suggested that if your baby is older than 18 months, "now would be a good time to start training him to adjust to sleeping under the pew!"

Do the Scriptures give us any guidelines in this area at all? Not a great deal is said about children in the congregation, but there are some passages that may help.

After the victory at Ai, all Israel gathered for a praise service. Joshua read to the people all the words of the Law (a very long service, indeed). It is interesting to notice who was there. Mentioned first are the elders, officers, and judges of Israel (Josh. 8:33). Then the *assembly of Israel* is further described (vs. 35) as including "the women and the little ones and the strangers who were living among them." Of special interest to us is the term translated *little ones*. It comes from a Hebrew root word meaning to walk with short, uncertain steps, or to toddle. The *little ones* were what we would call *toddlers*. Toddlers were included in the *assembly* when they came together to worship the Lord and to hear all the words of the Law.

In 2 Chronicles 20 Judah is invaded by an alliance of Moabites and Ammonites. King Jehoshaphat immediately declared a national emergency, and proclaimed a day of fasting and prayer throughout the kingdom. People from all the cities of Judah crowded into the Temple where Jehoshaphat himself led the great congregation in prayer. Verse 13 tells us that "all Judah was standing before the

Lord, with their infants, their wives, and their children."
Again we discover that infants (lit. toddlers) and older children were included among the worshippers. The Temple was
not *off-limits* to kids. They joined with the adults in hearing
the Word of God and in praying.

Nehemiah describes the worship of those who returned to
the land following the captivity in these words: "Then Ezra
the priest brought the law before the assembly of men,
women, and *all who could listen with understanding,* on the
first day of the seventh month" (Neh. 8:2). The latter term
is undoubtedly a reference to children who were present in
the congregation with the men and women. The format of
this service is similar to that in Joshua 8: the public reading
of the Law. Nehemiah further informs us that "all the people
were attentive to the book of the law," and this, *even though*
the service lasted from "early morning [first light] until
midday" (8:3).

These passages do not give to us any specific age when
children should be brought into the worship service, but
they do tell us that toddlers were part of the congregation
when the people gathered to praise the Lord and to hear His
Word. They also tell us that children did not come in order
to sleep under the pews! They came to worship the Lord,
even as others. Certainly they couldn't understand *everything*
that was going on, but as they were trained to be still, listen,
and join in whenever able, they experienced the reality of
corporate worship. As they grew in size and years, so did
their participation. They were not left out because they were
children.

When we come into the New Testament, we are immediately struck by the fact that our Lord Jesus always had time
for children, even though his disciples didn't think so. All
three synoptic gospels tell us of the time that the disciples
began to rebuke some parents who were bringing their

children to Jesus that He might bless them. Matthew and Mark both say that *children* were being brought to Him. Luke adds, "they were bringing even their *babies* [lit. nursing infants] to Him" (18:15). The disciples apparently thought that Christ was for grown-ups, not for kids. What a surprise when Jesus became *indignant* (Mark 10:14) and *rebuked them!* Brushing them aside, He took the little children in His arms and began blessing them.

The various letters, or *epistles,* of the New Testament were written and circulated in order to be read in all the churches when the people gathered to worship the Lord. It should not go unnoticed that the writers of these letters *expected* small children to be present in the congregation. In fact, in two of his letters the Apostle Paul even spoke especially and directly to them! Children in the cities of Ephesus and Colosse both received exhortations to obey their parents as their service to the Lord (Eph. 6:1; Col. 3:20). Apparently, as Paul wrote, he pictured the little faces that would be listening along with the adults and saved some words just for them.

Children should not be separated from the congregation: preachers should learn to sprinkle their sermons with instruction and application just for them. I am frankly afraid of church programs that fracture the congregation along the lines of age. If we have a generation gap, it's because we created it in Primary Church, Junior Church, and Senior Citizens' Services. What a beautiful sight it is to see old folks, young folks, and little folks lifting their voices *together* to praise the Lord.

But children need to be *trained* to worship. They won't naturally sit still and pay attention. How can we go about it? Let me offer a few suggestions.

At Juanita we have a *nursery* for children up to two years old. When they turn two they are promoted to the *training chapel.* The *training chapel* (formerly called the cry room) is located to the rear of the auditorium. A large picture window separates this room from the auditorium itself, and sound is piped in through a speaker. Here parents may train their toddlers to sit still and to pay attention. They are visually and audibly in touch with everything going on. The children may stand when we stand, sit when we sit, and make their *joyful noise* when we make ours—all without disturbing the main body of the congregation. If they need to stretch or stand up during the sermon, they can do it without disturbing anyone else. All the time they are learning that worship is for them too.

But the *training chapel* can't last forever! It is intended to be only a transitional stage. Usually within a few months the parents are ready to try their child in the *auditorium*. A sensitive congregation will reserve the back rows for parents with small children. Training is not completed yet, and emergency exits for discipline or bathroom are still very likely to be necessary, even though the children are learning to take care of their bathroom needs before the service begins. The major problem at this stage is for Mom and Dad to make the adjustment. They're uptight and super-sensitive to every wiggle and whisper. It's at this stage that the rest of us can really help.

If three-year-old Susie turns around and wrinkles up her pretty little nose at the people behind her, don't make faces back at her. She loves to play little games, and her games may keep someone five rows back from listening to the Word of God. But don't ignore her either. Using your index finger, silently signal her to turn around and pay attention. We don't have to tap her parents on the shoulder to tell them: they're already nervous enough. We don't want to *discourage* them; we want to *help* them.

What if Billy is downstairs tearing up a classroom while his parents are involved in a serious conversation with Elder

Jones? Should we interrupt that conversation to report on Billy's behavior? *"Mr. Smith, do you know what Billy's doing downstairs?"* *Obviously* he doesn't know what Billy is doing: if he did, Billy wouldn't be doing it! But should we break up what may be an intensely spiritual discussion in order to fetch Billy's parents? Why can't *we* stop Billy and tell him what he ought to be doing? We can always tell his parents later.

If the church is *really* a family under God, *then let's mean it.* Let's assume some responsibility and watch out for one another and our children. There's no reason for me to be offended if my brother or sister corrects my child in my absence: I ought to be thankful for the help. If a brother has to reprove my child while I'm standing right there I ought to be *embarrassed,* but *still* thankful for the help. I need all the real loving help I can get!

REVIEW

1. How is the behavior of our children a reflection of what we believe?
2. At what age did children participate in worship in the Old Testament?
3. What is the New Testament attitude?
4. Am I responsible to help other parents in my church with their children?

RESPONSE

1. Do my children participate in congregational worship? Why or why not?
2. What is the policy of my church on children in worship services?
3. Would a *training chapel* help the parents in our assembly?
4. If I saw Billy doing something destructive or dangerous, what would I do?

13

An Honest Confession

The principles developed in the preceding pages are both biblical and practical. When applied consistently, perseveringly, and properly, they will work. However, it is very important to remember that the perfect principles of the Word of God are to be poured through earthen vessels: imperfect parents.

Do you remember that correction is made necessary in the first place by the depraved and sinful nature of the child? We as parents are still a part of that same fallen humanity. Even though we have been redeemed by the grace of Jesus Christ, we must still wrestle against principalities, powers, and spiritual wickedness in high places. We must still struggle against sinful tendencies in our own lives. Luther said that sin is like a man's beard. You can shave it today, but it will be back again tomorrow.

This means that we must expect to fail, miserably and frequently, in our effort to implement biblical correction in our homes. Do not abandon the effort, for obedience always pays rich dividends in the end. Recognize that just as our children will fail to render perfect obedience because they are sinners, even so we will fail to render perfect correction because *we* are sinners. Yet even our imperfections and failures can be made to glorify God and edify our children if only we learn to handle them in a biblical manner.

There will be occasions when we will falsely accuse our children. It is deplorable, but it is unavoidable. Once my wife left our infant daughter strapped on the changing table while she deposited the *evidence* in the bathroom. Susanna's *big brother* was watching her. Suddenly there emerged a blood-curdling wail that brought me from the world of New Testament Greek into the nursery. There was Susanna, screaming—red with pain or rage or both. Nathan protested innocence, but we could find no evidence of anything that Susanna could have done to herself and concluded that Nathan must have poked his finger in her eye *by accident* (he's been known to do that). *Big brother* was guilty in the eyes of the law (me) and had to suffer the consequences for his alleged carelessness. Only later in the afternoon did my wife discover the telltale red scratch mark that was probably inflicted by Susanna's own little fingernail.

What would you do if you had wronged your little boy? Would you be afraid of losing your authority if you apologized to him? Remember that any authority we possess as parents is only delegated to us by God. If our children understand that *we* operate under God's authority the same as *they* do, then we have nothing to lose and everything to gain by confessing our sins to them whenever we wrong them. God's authority is established as being so great that even Dad dare not violate it without repentance, and our children see that we will not maintain the hypocritical double standard that prevails in so many homes. By confession of sin God is glorified and Dad gains the respect of his children.

What would you do? When I joined the family at dinner-time I reminded Nathan of what had happened earlier in the day and apologized for erroneously holding him to be at fault. Nathan knows that I am responsible to reflect the attitude of God in correction, but he also understands that I am a sinner saved by grace who occasionally fails miserably in fulfilling that responsibility.

It is almost impossible to overestimate the value and importance of setting the proper example for our children. J. C. Ryle ably reminds us:

> Instruction, and advice, and commands will profit little, unless they are backed up by the pattern of your own life. Your children will never believe you are in earnest, and really wish them to obey you, so long as your actions contradict your counsel. Archbishop Tillotson made a wise remark when he said, "To give children good instruction, and a bad example, is but beckoning to them with the head to show them the way to heaven, while we take them by the hand and lead them in the way to hell."

We all know or have parents who live by the philosophy "Do as I say and not as I do." If, as you fumble in your coat pocket for your matches, you say to Jimmy, "Never take up this dirty, nasty habit of smoking. If I ever catch you with a cigaret, I'll tan your hide!"—what impact will it have upon him? How disillusioned and disgusted he must be at the sight of such raw hypocrisy! How terribly ashamed his parents ought to be for the grievous crime they have committed against their son and against the Lord. As Christian parents, we must shun such open and obvious hypocrisy.

On the other hand, if you listened to *certain* preachers you would swear that Christian parents *rarely* sin, and certainly *never* before their children! How unreasonable and indeed unbiblical can one be? If we have taught our children that *all* have sinned and come short of the glory of God, then they already know that Mom and Dad are sinners just like everybody else! They *expect* Mom and Dad to sin, and are not surprised when we do. Indeed, if we are responsible to be examples to our children in all things, then that means that we are responsible to be examples to them in the area of sin and repentance as well.

I am *not* suggesting that we encourage our children to copy our sinful behavior patterns! I *am* saying that *when* we sin, we can be an example to our children in showing them how to deal with sin in their lives. They need to see, in a very realistic and visible way, how to handle frustration, anger, worry, and the other sins that crop up in the family context. If they have never seen us confessing sin, asking forgiveness, and making restitution, then we have failed to show them God's way of meeting the problems of daily living. We have failed to be examples to them in all things.

A man's home may be his castle, but a man cannot build walls strong enough to keep out those who live in the castle with him. Do you honestly believe that when you shut the bedroom door the children cannot tell that Mom and Dad are having another disagreement? Children can sense tension between their parents long before they can talk or even walk.

No, we are not perfect parents. We shall not be completely freed from sin until we are in the very presence of Jesus Christ, who shall appear the second time without sin unto salvation (Heb. 9:28). We are imperfect parents, creatures who will fight with our mates and wrong our children. We will falsely accuse them, prematurely judge them, unjustly afflict them, and unwittingly confuse them.

Notwithstanding all of this, if we will humbly seek to obey the Word of God as parents under God's authority—lovingly and consistently correcting our children when *they* fail, but honestly confessing our faults when *we* fail—we can powerfully influence our children by our holy example. Imperfect parents can nevertheless be godly parents! God always honors obedience to His commands.

REVIEW

1. Can only perfect parents be godly parents?

RESPONSE

1. In what specific areas do I fail to implement biblical correction in my home?
2. What can I do to change each problem noted above?
3. Do my children see me confessing my sins and asking their forgiveness when I'm wrong?

Appendices

1. Evangelizing Children

The relationship between discipline and evangelism is very close, for both are made necessary by the reality of sin. Every occasion for discipline is an opportunity to point our children to God as their Creator and to Christ as the only Redeemer. Every day provides us with many such opportunities.

What shall we tell our children? Always the truth. We need to tell them about the Fall and about its effect upon all of us. We need to tell them that they're sinners. Sometimes when we ask our child why he did something, he replies, "I don't know." And he *really doesn't* understand why. We must tell him biblically why it is true that "foolishness is bound up in the heart of a child" (Prov. 22:15). We need to tell them about Christ and the cross, about the new birth, faith, and repentance. We need to tell them some really basic things about who God is and what He does. Many years ago Andrew Bonar said, "We tell them, 'You are sinners, exposed to God's wrath and curse, and you cannot save yourselves; but God's own Son can save you, by Himself bearing that wrath and curse.'" We tell them the whole Gospel.

When they respond to the gospel command and profess to believe in Christ, how can we evaluate their profession? Here are some things to remember:

1. *In a sense* I will never be *fully satisfied* with my own child's profession of faith until he establishes his own household and perseveres in pressing on. As long as he is under my roof, I will never know with absolute confidence whether his faith and obedience is in response to Christ, or to me. Children are under a great deal of pressure to conform to the expectations of other people (parents, teacher, pastor, Sunday School teacher, etc.). We need to be very careful that we do not encourage a *false* profession.

2. Children are capable of regeneration, and therefore of conversion. Christianity is for kids as well as for adults, and the Lord does save many as children.

3. But a child's way of expressing repentance and faith will not be nearly so precise, knowledgeable, or sophisticated as the testimony of an adult. Children are children, and must be allowed to express themselves in their own way. We cannot demand that children speak the religious language of adults.

4. Yet there *will be* certain evidences of the saving work of Christ.
   a. Look for a *spontaneous interest* in the things of Christ. When children are found engaged in spiritual activities because *they want to,* and not merely because *their parents say to,* there is ground for real hope.
   b. Look for *expressions of simple love* and devotion to the Savior.
   c. Look for a *willingness to be conformed* to the scriptural expectations of them as children. Christian children are not perfect any more than Christian adults are perfect. But they will generally want to obey the Lord and their parents.

2. The Rod and Correction

I will be a father to him and he will be a son to Me; when he commits iniquity, I will correct him with the rod of men and the strokes of the sons of men (2 Sam. 7:14).

Then I will visit their transgression with the rod, and their iniquity with stripes (Ps. 89:32).

On the lips of the discerning, wisdom is found, but a rod is for the back of him who lacks understanding (Prov. 10:13).

He who spares his rod hates his son, but he who loves him disciplines him diligently (Prov. 13:24).

In the mouth of the foolish is a rod for his back, but the lips of the wise will preserve them (Prov. 14:3).

Foolishness is bound up in the heart of a child; the rod of discipline will remove it far from him (Prov. 22:15).

Do not hold back discipline from the child, although you beat him with the rod, he will not die (Prov. 23:13).

You shall beat him with the rod, and deliver his soul from Sheol (Prov. 23:14).

A whip is for the horse, a bridle for the donkey, and a rod for the back of fools (Prov. 26:3).

The rod and reproof give wisdom, but a child who gets his own way brings shame to his mother (Prov. 29:15).

Woe to Assyria, the rod of My anger, and the staff in whose hand is My indignation (Isa. 10:5).

I am the man who has seen affliction because of the rod of His wrath (Lam. 3:1).

What do you desire? Shall I come to you with a rod or with love and a spirit of gentleness? (1 Cor. 4:21).

3. Parents' Topical Reference

This listing of topics and appropriate Scripture passages is only intended to get you started. We have left sufficient space for you to add additional topics and verses to use with your children.

I. *General disobedience*

> Exod. 20:12
> Eph. 6:1, 2
> Col. 3:20

II. *Specific sins*

> *Anger*

>> Gen. 4:1-8
>> Ps. 37:8

Prov. 14:17, 29; 15:1, 18; 16:32; 17:14; 19:11, 19;
20:3; 22:24, 25; 25:28; 29:11; 30:33
Matt. 5:21, 22
Mark 3:5
Eph. 4:26-32
James 1:19, 20; 4:1-3

Attitude

Gen. 4:1-7
Prov. 25:28
1 Cor. 14:30-32
Gal. 5:22, 23
2 Peter 1:5-9

Cheating (see Stealing)

Communication

Eph. 4:25-32

Confession

Prov. 28:13
James 5:16
1 John 1:9

Drunkenness

>   Prov. 20:1; 23:20, 21, 29-35
>   Eph. 5:18

Envy

>   Ps. 37:1-11
>   Prov. 3:31; 14:30 (AV); 23:17; 24:1, 19; 27:4
>   Song of Sol. 8:6
>   James 3:14-16
>   1 Peter 2:1, 2

Forgiveness

>   Matt. 6:14, 15; 18:15-17, 21-35
>   Eph. 4:32
>   Col. 3:13
>   1 John 1:8-10

Friendship

>   Prov. 17:9, 17; 18:24; 22:24-25; 25:17; 27:6, 9, 10,
>   17
>   Eccles. 4:9-12
>   Amos 3:3 (AV)

John 15:13-15
1 Cor. 15:33

Homosexuality

Gen. 19
Lev. 18:22; 20:13
Rom. 1:26-32
1 Cor. 6:9-11
1 Tim. 1:8-11

Hope

Prov. 10:28; 19:18
Rom. 15:4, 5
Heb. 6:11, 17-19

Humility

Prov. 15:33; 16:19; 22:4; 29:23
Phil. 2:1-11
1 Peter 5:6, 7

Laziness

   Prov. 6:6-11; 12:24; 13:4; 15:19; 18:9; 20:4; 24:30-
       34; 26:13-16
   Matt. 25:26
   2 Thess. 3:6-12

Lying

   Exod. 20:16
   Ps. 52:1-4; 58:3
   Prov. 6:16-19; 12:19, 22
   Eph. 4:25
   Col. 3:9
   Rev. 21:8

Listening

   Prov. 1:8; 2:1-5; 5:1, 2; 13:18; 15:31; 18:13; 23:22,
       23; 29:1

Name-calling

   Matt. 5:21, 22
   James 3:9, 10

Obedience

Exod. 20:12
1 Sam. 15:22
Acts 4:18-20; 5:29
Eph. 6:1, 2
Phil. 2:8
Col. 3:20
Heb. 5:8; 13:17

Pride

Prov. 6:16-18; 8:13; 11:2; 13:10; 16:5, 18, 19; 18:
    11, 12; 21:4; 25:27; 27:2; 28:25
Mark 7:20-23
Rom. 12:3
1 Cor. 4:5-7; 10:12
Gal. 6:3
1 Tim. 3:6
James 4:6

Reconciliation

Matt. 5:23-25; 18:15-17
Luke 17:3-5
Eph. 4:31, 32

Repentance

    2 Chron. 7:14
    Neh. 1:9
    Ps. 51
    Prov. 28:13
    Isa. 55:6, 7
    Mark 2:17
    Luke 15:7; 18:13, 14
    Acts 2:38; 3:19; 5:31; 17:30
    2 Cor. 7:9, 10
    1 Thess. 1:9

Reproof

    Lev. 19:17
    Ps. 141:5
    Prov. 6:23; 9:8, 9; 10:17; 12:1; 13:18; 15:5, 10, 31,
        32; 17:10; 25:12; 27:5, 6; 28:23; 29:15
    Matt. 18:15-17
    Luke 17:3-5
    1 Tim. 5:1, 2, 20

Resentment

    Prov. 26:24-26
    Heb. 12:15

Restitution

    Exod. 21:28-36; 22:1-15
    Lev. 6:1-5
    Num. 5:6, 7
    Prov. 6:30, 31
    Ezek. 33:15, 16
    Luke 19:8, 9

Stealing

    Exod. 20:15
    Lev. 19:11
    Deut. 23:24, 25
    Prov. 6:30, 31; 28:24; 29:24; 30:7-9
    Jer. 7:9-11
    Matt. 6:19, 20
    Rom. 2:21
    Eph. 4:28

Talebearing

    Lev. 19:16
    Ps. 15:1-3
    Prov. 11:13; 16:28; 17:9; 18:8; 20:19; 26:20-22

Talking back (to parents)

Exod. 20:12; 21:15, 17
Deut. 21:18-21

Acknowledgement: The *idea* for including a list such as this came from *The Use of the Scriptures in Counseling* by Jay Adams; (Presbyterian & Reformed Publishing Co., 1975).